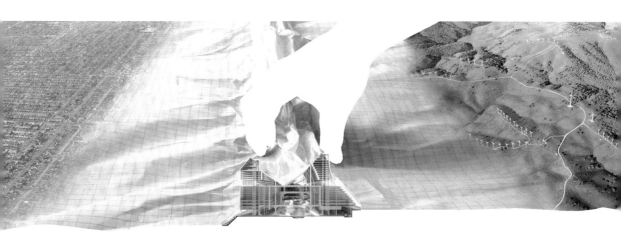

Cosanti Press, Mayer, AZ, 86333, USA
www.arcosanti.org

This publication was made possible through support provided by
Ecoculture Foundation, Yangpyeong, Korea.

Printed in the United States of America
Book design and graphics: Youngsoo Kim
Cover design: Tomiaki Tamura and Youngsoo Kim

ISBN 978-1-883340-07-0
Library of Congress Control Number: 2011927989

Lean Linear City: Arterial Arcology

Paolo Soleri
Youngsoo Kim
Charles Anderson
Adam Nordfors
Scott Riley
Tomiaki Tamura

Foreword by Jeff Stein · Edited by Youngsoo Kim · Text edited by Lissa McCullough

Cosanti Press

Lean Linear City: Arterial Arcology

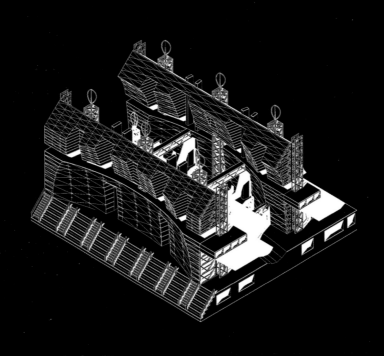

Contents

Foreword 8
Jeff Stein

Lean Linear City 12

Lean Alternative 84

Miniaturization-Complexity 102

Arcology 114

Arterial Arcology 138

Lean Linear City as an Arterial Arcology 142
Tomiaki Tamura

Density and Transportation Systems of Lean Linear City 148
Youngsoo Kim

Neo-Nature and the Evolution of Space 160
Adam Nordfors

Lean Linear City Landscape 174
Charles Anderson

Cognition of Urban Space 180
Scott Riley

References and Credits 188

About the Authors 190

Index 192

Foreword

Welcome to an important exploration of architectural and cultural thinking and design. Based on the pioneering work of architect Paolo Soleri, what you are about to read unfolds a collaborative new investigation of Soleri's idea for a Lean Linear City. In these pages architecture and ecology confront the necessity to reformulate how we inhabit the planet to create a complex and immanent solution for the future of the city. In addition to examining the design and methodology for creating an event of such enormous complexity, this book also elaborates why we must do it.

Humans want to connect—to each other, to goods, services, ideas. It is why most of us alive on the planet now live in cities: the city is the best instrument we have devised to make these connections. But we also want—and need—to connect to nature, to the earth itself, and to that bit of the earth's ecology we do not control. And we need to design ways to do that without overwhelming what remains of the earth's natural systems, habitats, and landscapes.

This book describes a new parameter for design: leanness. It is based on a clear understanding of how life on earth functions. As the authors point out, because of our population numbers, because of the attitude we have taken until now about how to design and develop our cities, we are in some difficulty as a species. We have placed every other species on the earth into some difficulty, too. A reformulated, lean design of the kind described in these pages could very well be how we get out of it.

Architecture historian Christian Norburg Schulz points out that humans are "wanderers by nature, always on the way." On the other hand, when we do settle and identify with a certain place, the result is architecture. Soleri's arterial arcology shows how we can reconcile this dichotomy of human life on earth, the dialectic of departure and return—path and goal—that characterizes our place in the world. While our current urban culture has been able to provide the civilizing comforts of buildings, possessions, and literacy, it has yet to integrate these static comforts with the nomad in us, the part that is in love with movement.

To relate architecture and cities to their citizens, to an audience in motion, designers must make architecture work harder, designing buildings—and cities—to be leaner, more like living things, integral parts of a living landscape, able to engage human senses beyond the merely visual. This emphasis on lean urban performance while carrying forth a new understanding of urban form characterizes the work of arterial arcology.

This book comes to us at a watershed moment, when the very basis of culture and economy, and thus our relationship with each other and the cosmos, is being re-thought and requires re-thinking. A Japanese term for this is *hashi*: the end of one thing and beginning of another. *Hashi* can describe a bridge, chopsticks, or a book like this.

Lean Linear City: Arterial Arcology, in this *hashi* moment, presents some of the most important designs yet made for understanding the coming relationship of people, place, and planet. I hope its publication will spark action among its readers, so that we can take our rightful place as humans on the earth, one species among many others, truly extra-ordinary in what we are becoming.

Welcome to the real work of the next generation, and to the lean, linear blueprint for how we can go about that work.

Jeff Stein, AIA
President, Cosanti Foundation

Lean Linear City extending through the countryside

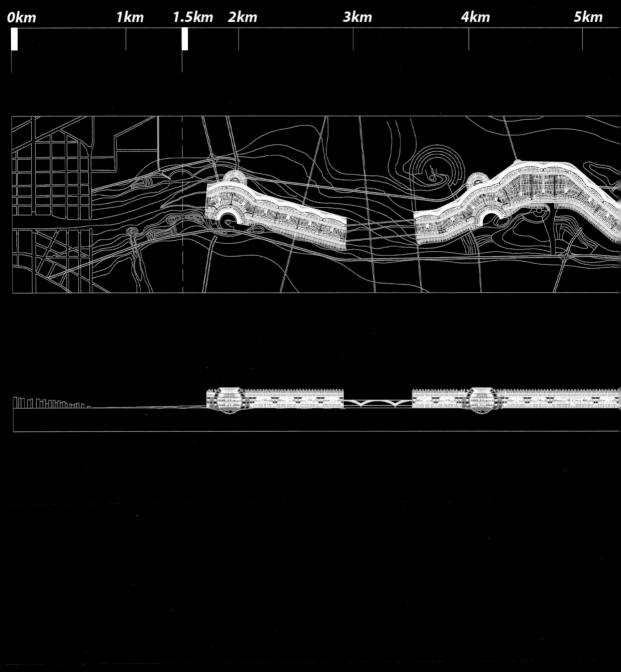

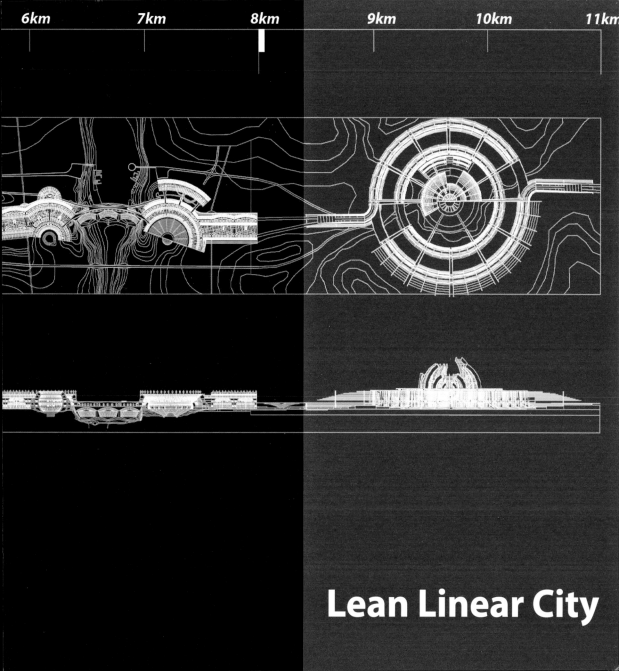

6km 7km 8km 9km 10km 11km

Lean Linear City

IN 2010, MORE THAN 50%
of world population lived in urban areas

= 3.5 BILLION

BY 2050, 6.3 BILLION
are projected to live in urban areas

Source: United Nations Department of Economic and Social Affairs, Population Division, *World Urbanization Prospects*, 2009 revision, New York, 2010

Unlimited urban sprawl produces the land of the hermits, that is, of unavoidable segregation-loneliness. Cities, which are urban effects, are cultural instruments that require the awareness of life cultivating the self-awareness of *Homo sapiens*. The city is where the "me" of the hermit is elevated into the "us" of the species. The hermit of exurbia is operating in an evolutionary vacuum.

For architecture to metamorphose into a coherent human ecology, a reformulation is necessary that puts distance between it and our present reigning materialism. The trend, however, has been overwhelmingly in the opposite direction. The metastasis of the city in the forms of suburbia and exurbia has been implementing what I call a "planetary hermitage." The American dream of giving each persona, isolated in his or her home, all that is needed for self-sufficiency feeds a monumental delusion, a direct route to degenerating the human persona, the space it controls, and the planet. The immense consumption of resources needed to build the "dream" and keep it running has had no equivalent on this planet.

The "global village" promoted by architects, developers, and speculators is turning out instead to be a planetary hermitage. This is probably the most dramatic demonstration of lost coherence today: the progressive, ceaseless, mindless construction of the planetary hermitage, that is, the de facto segregation of the smallest social grouping, the family (or the fragments of it that remain), into its own private walled-in enclave, defended if necessary with firearms.

There is horizontal hermitage and there is vertical hermitage. In the typical profile of today's cities there is the central forest of very tall buildings with their top elite enclosed in a hermitage scaffolding. Then there is the totality of the city per se, ringed by the single-home hermitages radiating unendingly over what was formerly farmland.

The moment is critical for urban innovations, given the intense industriousness manifest in China, India, Latin America, and other regions of the world, now adopting the endless America-inspired hermitages of suburbia and exurbia. The metastasis of the city in the form of suburban and exurban developments, the most pernicious of our intrusions into the environment, is the industry of a "better kind of wrongness" pursued on a planetary scale. We, along with the whole of life, suffer from this opaqueness.

China at night,
Beijing–Tianjin, China,
NASA photograph, 2010

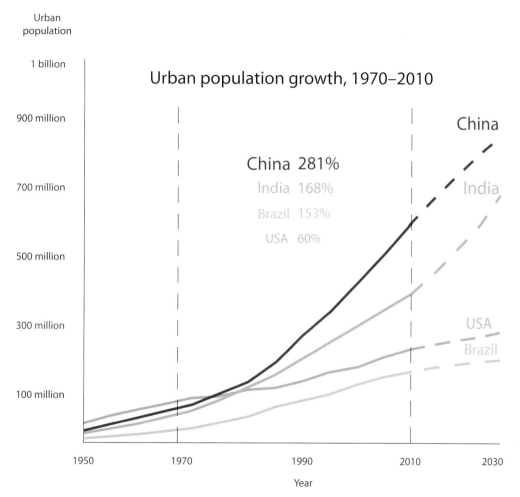

Urban population growth, 1970–2010

China 281%
India 168%
Brazil 153%
USA 60%

China
India
USA
Brazil

Urban population

1 billion
900 million
700 million
500 million
300 million
100 million

1950 1970 1990 2010 2030

Year

Source: United Nations, *World Urbanization Prospects*, 2007 revision

China, on the border of a new era, has the enviable chance to leap above technocratic culture and land in a quasi-pristine environment with a post-Western formula. The Western formula is showing signs of hitting the wall of unconditional materialism, herald by what the American dream is turning out to be. To reform this landscape is an exercise in too little too late. Reform will not affect mankind differently, because it works at improving the wrong thing and thus moves toward a dead end.

Urban area growth in Shenzen, China, 1979–2005:

450%

894.31 km²

19.55 km²

Source: Zhi-qiang Lv et al., "Monitoring of urban sprawl using geoprocessing tools in the Shenzhen municipality, China," 2010

5 miles   Manhattan   San Francisco   Rome   Paris

Shenzhen urban growth, 1979–2005

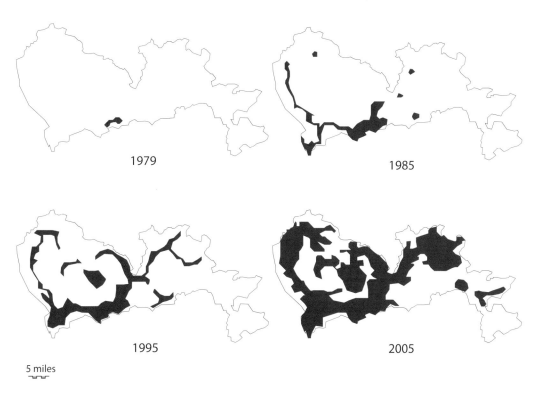

1979

1985

1995

2005

5 miles

Source: Zhi-qiang Lv et al., "Monitoring of urban sprawl using geoprocessing tools in the Shenzhen municipality, China," 2010

Migrations, invasions, and resettlements have long been part of the human presence on the planet, but ultimately we have established patterns of settled populations. It seems, however, that the prevailing mode of settled population is undergoing technologically driven alterations. Mobility is becoming fashionable. Millions of people are flying hundreds and thousands of miles daily for work, reunions, and leisure. In the next era we are "transported," meaning we are transporting ourselves and our baggage from here to there, no longer only out of curiosity or in quest of experience, but also as a manner of living. We leave in order to live. So perhaps the city had better adapt and adopt? The city as a traveling urban phenomenon: the linear city.

The success of the merchant is directly proportional to the intensity and success of the movement of people going places—not exclusively to the marketplace. No great imagination is needed to expand, intensify, enrich the milieu of the commerce road into a full-fledged urban-effect condition that wraps around the traffic, so to speak, the modest means to "make a living," and becomes the river of civilization and culture, if such ambition is solicited by the linear concentration of the living, learning, producing, and merchandizing of creatures of conviviality, from schools to libraries, health centers, museums, laboratories, loci of leisure and transportation.

We must inject mobility into the urban context. I propose the linear city as one radical alternative rooted in the parallel running of the urban phenomenon and the logistics intrinsic to its becoming. Lean Linear channels both the physical and the hyperphysical (civilizational and cultural) presence in self-contained complexes and intense urban ribbons capable of lining the continent in the leanest possible mode. As such, it may respond to some of the critical situations now taking form in China, and soon in India. A continent as populated as China on the brink of hyperconsumerism cannot afford to engulf its farmland with parkways, highways, roads, parking lots, garages, and dumpsites. These are consequences of the unchecked metastasis of the city into suburbia and exurbia.

A large proportion of life is spent delivering and retrieving things: the disposal and reuse of resources required by life. Life is a logistical problem; that is, life is howness.

Taipei, 2005

Los Angeles, 2007

Logistics are servosystems intimately connected with the life systems they travel in, distributing and retrieving. Recognizing that it is impossible to emulate the logistical sophistication that organisms (vegetal, animal, fungal) have opportunistically invented in pursuit of survival and reproduction, we must try to understand some of their ways, for theirs is an unequalled record of logistical efficiency. Cardinal for them are two factors: (1) Extraordinary use of space, which I call the "urban effect," a multilayered interacting of highly discriminatory performances, the gist of rich life. (2) A stringent economy and the indispensable synergistic comings and goings conducive to exchange of information and knowledge.

Anything that moves, from red corpuscles in the blood to the raging folly of galaxies, is logistics in action. This means that medical internists and astronomers are colleagues in pursuing key formulas for grasping an ever-metamorphosing space.

Energy is the geometry of space present in all transportation-cargo operations, from red corpuscles to a New York stage to household gadgetries. For all of those transportation and storage dilemmas, the flat exurbia is as realistic as a flat planet, a parallel reality of our fabrication. To evidence the folly of flat suburbia, wish away the overt and intended grounds of exurbia to uncover the intricate scatterization structures feeding and maintaining the single-unit homes for hundreds of square miles.

Once again, we do well not to go after the effect, the universalized hermitage itself, but after the syndrome that produces this effect: that is, populations in a state of chronic segregation. When it comes to the social-human nexus, the "solution" is not speed and the wheel. The "solution" is proximity; gravity tells us so, and gravity is the disciplinarian of all. The prime shaper of the planet and its evolution is gravity. Gravity causes its sphericity, and gravity is the unavoidable intruder in every aspect, function, and performance of all things belonging to that sphere. Physiologically, we are molded by gravity that weighs in the microscopic, macroscopic, and megascopic. It has issued us our limbs to walk with (the artful biped, now an endangered species?). A planet with a fraction of Earth's gravity would have developed creatures we could not identify, let alone recognize as familiar.

It takes

2 train cars
max capacity 120

4 buses
max capacity 60

60 cars
max capacity 4

to move 240 people

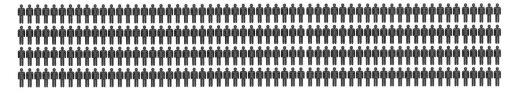

Gravity, one of the major makers of our presence, is as fully present in habitat as it is in the whole logistic of life. A better awareness of this fact would go a long way in making our logistics less extravagant, explaining to us why we are the way we are, and clarifying our need for a habitat coherent with gravity. To move things large and small takes labor, which is to say, energy; that is why proximity becomes the right avenue to the door of knowledge and performance.

The realism and coherence of transport in its five dimensionality—the three coordinates of space, plus time and energy—are five variations of space geometries.

In the macro reality we hominids have become, the logistics of daily life have grown exponentially, courtesy of passionate *Homo faber* (man the maker), full of pride for his novel industrialized landscapes. We must reformulate the cultural-civic deserts of exurbia into lively centers for culture, commerce, and the arts by way of urban nodes conjoined by urban ribbons (such as Lean Linear), reliable in terms of supporting learning, leisure, productivity, markets. In addition and most important, the same structures should produce energy and be logistical conveyors, starting from the pedestrian on up (or down?).

The largest sector of infrastructure is the one dealing with logistics. Life depends on logistics of distribution and disposal. As a living cell is an extraordinary set of micrologistics, so a megacity is an extraordinary set of macrologistics. The logistics of contemporary industrialized man are extremely inefficient and wasteful, as our traffic gridlocks and dumpsites testify. Maintaining and improving these modes only modifies what is dysfunctional—a too conservative approach that epitomizes what I call a "better kind of wrongness."

Mere reform falls short of the task of facing and coping with the new conditions generated by our industriousness, given that it is mostly the attempt to improve what exists, producing only a better kind of wrongness. The task we face is one of reformulation—a daunting task, and an inevitable one. The radicalism of reformulation implies a gradualist approach: laboratory-like institutes working on urban problems step-by-step and functioning as testing grounds for the nonsegregational attack that the problems demand.

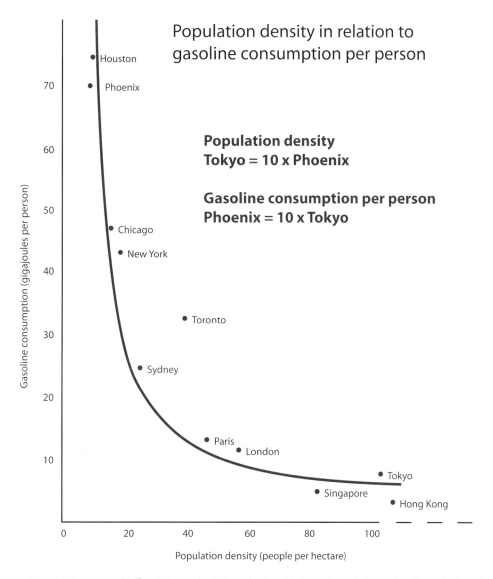

Population density in relation to gasoline consumption per person

Population density Tokyo = 10 x Phoenix

Gasoline consumption per person Phoenix = 10 x Tokyo

Source: Peter W. G. Newman and Jeffrey R. Kenworthy, *Cities and Automobile Dependence: An International Sourcebook*, 1989

The inefficient logistical reticulum of our industrialized nation needs to be reformulated from the ground up. As the logistical infrastructure now in disrepair is obsolete anyway, we need a serious conceptual reformulation of the whole system along realistic guidelines, not futilely fighting the ever-increasing congestion of roads, highways, and parking areas by expanding roadways to accommodate ever-increasing traffic, but reformulating the damaging patterns of our communities, especially our anticultural, anti-environmental, antisocial promulgation of one- to two-story single-family homes. One house or mansion per family requires a logistical landscape horrendously wasteful and brutally anti-environmental—the antithesis of greenness.

Here the word "reformulation"—to form again—refers to the imperative to reformulate intentions that per se are no longer coherent but constitute a race into capriciousness, self-contradiction, inequity, destruction, collapse, nemesis.

A reformulation of our self-creational élan requires the quarantine of the suburban "hermitage" and a total reformulation of our "greenness," compromised as it is now by *Homo faber* materialism. If it is impossible to redirect the tide by means of reform, it is possible and necessary to propose total reformulation. Here is where the hope of the true green resides.

A lean alternative to hyperconsumption becomes an imperative: we need a genuine reformulation of the human presence, the human ecology, starting with our most basic needs—shelter and food. Curbing hyperconsumption in favor of a lean alternative implies that *Homo faber* works in the service of *Homo sapiens*. The doings of man face precariousness as a fact of life, but that very precariousness gives self-creation the fiber necessary to create that which does not exist, to transcend what now exists, and to give intensive and novel purpose to the evolutionary feat of life.

Success is mandated by opportunism within the bewildering complexity of the present human context; no one brain has within its own bewildering spatial geometries a sufficient knowledge to outline the next step, let alone implement the new ascent expected from self-creation.

Phoenix, Arizona,
USA, 2005

Manhattan,
New York City, 2005

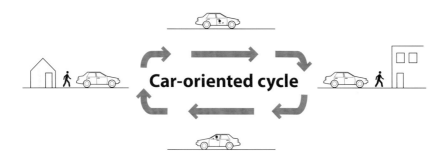

Car-oriented cycle

The typical suburban commuting cycle bypasses many aspects of the urban commuting cycle, reducing social contacts and cultural opportunities in the course of daily life.

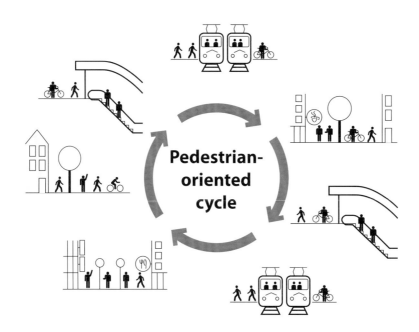

Pedestrian-oriented cycle

Phoenix, Arizona, USA, 2005

Hong Kong, China, 2005

The need is to consider and weigh any serious conjecture nourished by commitments that go far beyond the political and financial vested interests of the moment. That means to insert our thinking and doing in the historical progression human beings have been authoring coherently within the evolutionary tide we are co-authoring. This requires an action that goes far beyond the usually compromising posture that is satisfying to the conservative instinct of our species (in common with other animal species).

If, of the three or so billion adults living on the planet, I am alone in thinking the way I do, chances are pretty high that I am wrong. So be it. I must add, "What if…?" A reformulation is a declaration, a formula for potential action, whereas a movement is actual transformational action. A reformulation can be a personal proposal; a movement entails multitudes, and one is never a multitude.

The largest sector of infrastructure needing reformulation is the one dealing with logistics and its far-reaching presence in all aspects of life. It might turn out that human habitat has to be realigned with the logistical grids serving it. That requires urban ribbons of modest width incorporating parallel roads, cycling pathways, public-transit services, and stations for local, regional, and continental trains. Transversal to the urban ribbon, the servosystems complete the logistical grid.

I have developed Lean Linear Arterial arcology as an elongation of the arcology principle intended to perform well with respect to the main logistical reticulum now so indispensable to urban life. Lean Linear is the study of an urban environ along the main logistical systems existent or anticipated. The main promise of leanness consists in an unflagging thrust toward a recoordination of cultures within and along intense broad-ranging experiences available, as history tells us, only in urban coordinations. As we are definers of spaces and are defined by space, the natural environ and the manmade environs, the lean linear city is a conjecture willing to test and improve different geometries of space.

Process of urban sprawl

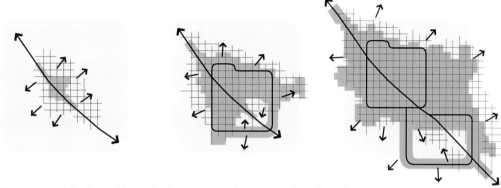

The automobile-based logistical system works as a catalyst for urban expansion, energy consumption, and environmental impact.

Lean Linear process

The mass-transit based logistical system works implosively to contain urban sprawl, marginalize energy consumption, and limit environmental impact.

"Mobility" is one of the virtues we prize and iconize in the present way of life. It might be smart to recognize: first, the stupefying ways organisms achieve complexity when the arterial–venous logistic is applied, and second, the no less stupefying leanness of those logistics, as life is channeled by arteries. The residuals of life processes are channeled by a virtually symmetrical set of veins. The artery–vein system is a world of fluidity, flexibility, responsiveness, emergence, reliability. And the versatile pump, the heart, is another performing singularity serving zillions of tenants. Our cumbersome, uncoordinated, segregative, materialistic, idolized, hyperconsumptive systems desperately need the best logistical network we can concoct. They must emulate the self-reliant, self-disciplined, nonsegregational lean reticulum, proven by the success of evolution.

Lean Linear, an arterial arcology, proposes a dense and continuous urban ribbon designed to take advantage of regional wind patterns and solar radiation, both photovoltaic and greenhouse. Thus energy-wise it is optimally suited for breezy and sunny regions. The habitat "coincides" with logistical channels by incorporating the means of transit within the societal presence, that is, hyperlogistics within hyperurban structures.

Indifference to climactic cycles and 24-hour cycles in air and temperature translates into indifference in energy consumption, pollution, equipment wear, and necessarily the collective swelling of push-button materialism. We have two choices: to work with air, solar, and temperature variations or remain indifferent to them. The push-button consumerist society chooses indifference. By contrast, how best to harness a portion of solar and wind energy, now that fossil fuels are beginning to show signs of exhaustion, is essential to the proposed linear city's structural and functional morphology.

Lean Linear is energized by means of two continuous photovoltaic bands, as well as two continuous bands of wind generators and greenhouses. They are integral elements of the Lean Linear structure, providing a significant percentage of energy needs, diminishing dependence on high voltage national grids, and capable of protecting and sustaining the life of the city in times of emergency (tsunami, hurricane, tornado, flood, and the like.)

Mobility / Density diagram

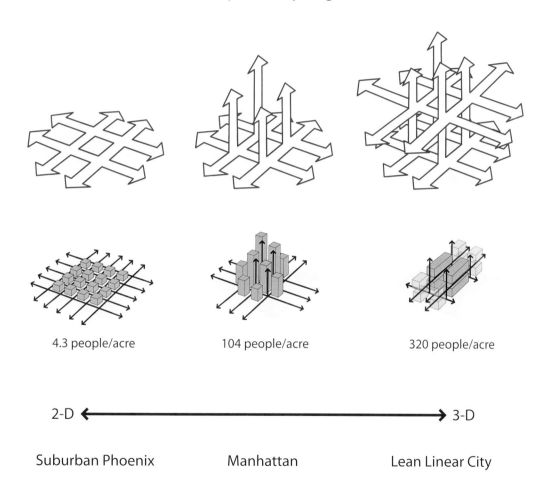

4.3 people/acre

104 people/acre

320 people/acre

2-D ⟷ 3-D

Suburban Phoenix

Manhattan

Lean Linear City

According to preliminary projections, each "module" of the city measuring 200 meters in length accommodates about 3,000 residents and the spaces for productive, commercial, institutional, cultural, recreational, and health activities. In a matter of a few minutes the pedestrian can reach most of the locations in his or her daily routine. In a matter of a few more minutes walking, cycling, or using public conveyors such as trains, he or she can reach the adjacent "town," or urban module, to the left or the right.

Most of the locomotion would be sheltered by greenhouse or parasol but not separated from the open air, the indoor–outdoor alternatives of the Central Park. The park running on the central axis of Lean Linear is an uninterrupted green landscape with a climate free from the extremes of cold and heat because it is a multistory greenhouse with a "roof" that is transparent to the sun in the cold season and parasol-like in the warm-hot season.

Each module is designed to collect a percentage of its energy needs on the spot, in addition to providing staple foods, such as fruits and vegetables, harvested from the greenhouse aprons spreading down the southerly elevation and the terraced orchards on the northerly elevation. At the lower ends of the greenhouse aprons, the short skirt of "suburbia" develops. The skirt must be a tutu: rigorously contained suburban spread could develop on a fascia no wider than one kilometer, so as to accommodate travel by public transportation, cycle, and foot. The private automobile would be rigorously confined to auxiliary functions (outings, research, etc.).

In five minutes on the train you could traverse ten "mini provinces" (modules), each with its own distinctive flavor, akin to New York's ethnic neighborhoods. The variations available for the single module to "reinvent" itself are unlimited, given the ingenuity and resolve of the planners, designers, and populations involved. The modular characteristics could not be mandated; rather they would have to come about as the city started to click as a lean, continuous human habitat. Such an astonishing lineup of provinces is only conceivable with a highly efficient and swift logistical support. Once the provinces are splintered from common logistics, what remains are civic asphyxiation, societal paralysis, starvation, and death.

Lean Linear City module development study

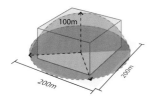

5-min walking distance:
200m x 200m x 100m

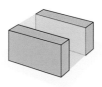

Park space:
open space
between two
main structures

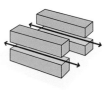

Terra level:
pedestrian and
local transit system

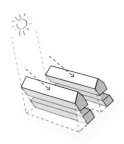

Solar angle:
optimum angle for
photovoltaic panels and
passive solar strategy

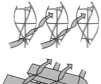

Wind movement:
wind turbines and
cross-ventilation strategy

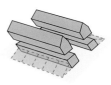

Urban agriculture:
local food production
supporting the urban
community

Lean Linear City module plan and elevation

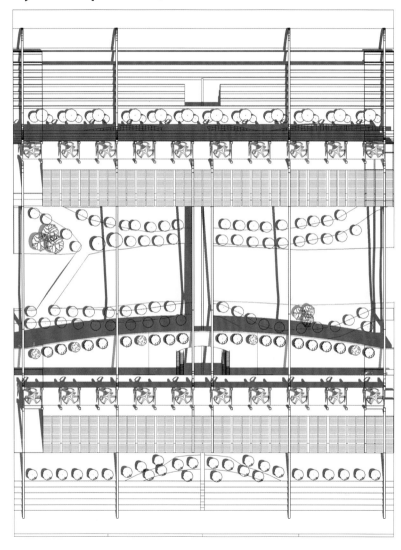

Lean Linear City
module plan

N

0 10 20 30 40 50m

200m

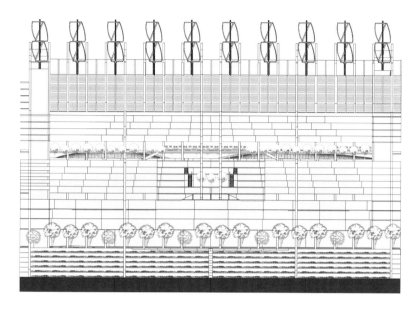

Lean Linear City
south elevation

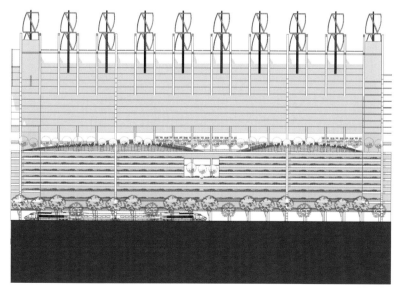

Lean Linear City
north elevation

200m

0   10   20   30   40   50m

37

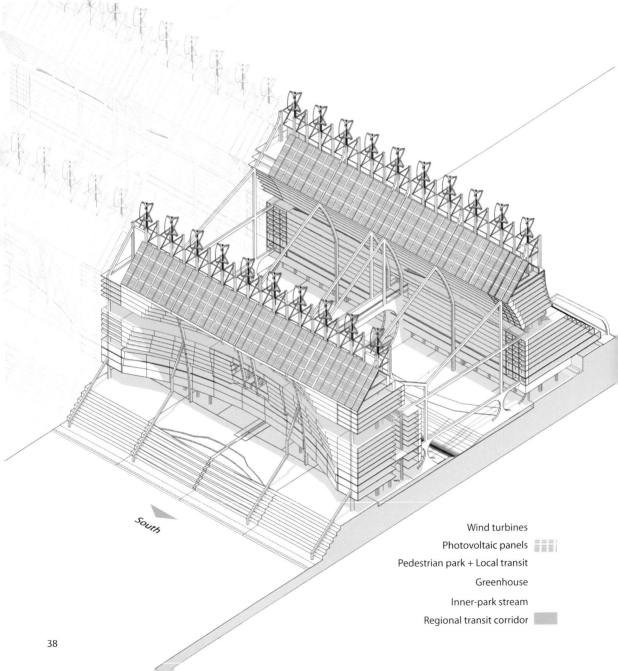

South

Wind turbines

Photovoltaic panels

Pedestrian park + Local transit

Greenhouse

Inner-park stream

Regional transit corridor

Lean Linear City module features

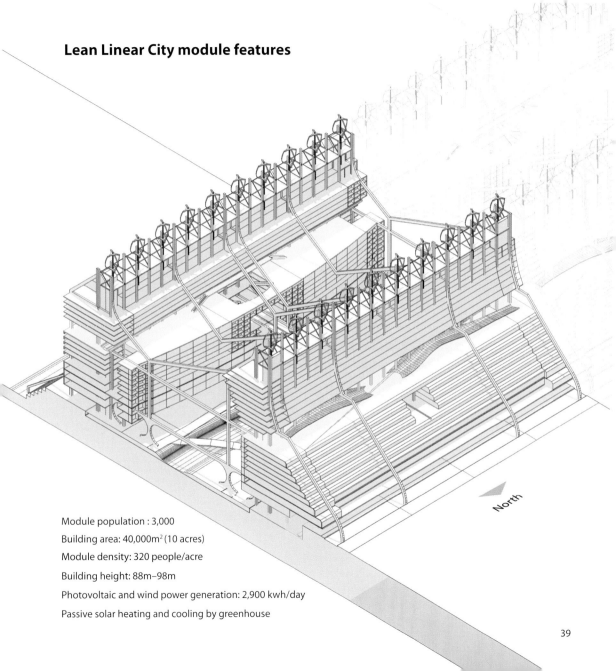

North

Module population : 3,000

Building area: 40,000m² (10 acres)

Module density: 320 people/acre

Building height: 88m–98m

Photovoltaic and wind power generation: 2,900 kwh/day

Passive solar heating and cooling by greenhouse

Although a single module of Lean Linear (3,000 residents) is a relatively modest urban enterprise, a fully developed lean urban ribbon (extending tens or hundreds of kilometers) would be able to employ a very large, skilled, and diverse labor pool. In the module, all the internal arterial systems open themselves to the two analogous systems in the modules to the right and left—and suddenly things get moving. The inner arterial movement of a conventional town, with its blind alleys and gridwork gyrations, would flow into a larger stream interlinked with other urban modules. The city "moving" to bring itself across the open land for residents that thus become simultaneously city dwellers (in the linear city) and country dwellers (in the adjacent land).

All the vertebrate organisms of the planet, zillions of them evolving for thousands of years, are the investment of the flesh on one and only one skeletal structure. The way the evolution of an extraordinary variety of vertebrates has been plied on one and only one skeletal geometry suggests an analogous and emulative possibility, if we transpose organic structural geometry into the inorganic geometries of planning and architecture. This is even more plausible when a proposed alternative is at its initial formulation. I have adopted a skeletal diagram for Lean Linear that enables a number of functions to work together. A desegregation and reintegration of sorts, and in addition an access to photovoltaic-eolic energy captured and used on the spot.

Homologous vertebrate structures and variations

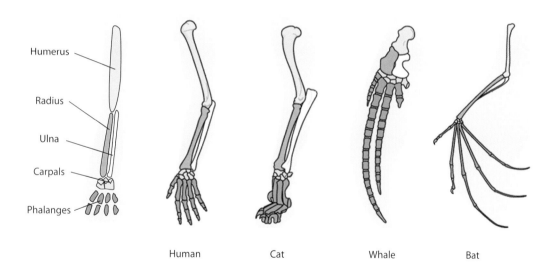

Humerus
Radius
Ulna
Carpals
Phalanges

Human   Cat   Whale   Bat

The physical structure of Lean Linear is neutral concerning the "coloratura" that characterizes and historicizes all human settlements. It antedates them while anticipating the leanness so critical for the evolution of *Homo faber–Homo sapiens*, all of us. Interiors are left to the intervention of "local" architects and designers, introducing the ethnicity proper to the location of the modules. Its basic "skeleton" is composed of structural elements of size, weight, and reciprocal anchorages, whereas the arcological modules of Lean Linear can "travel" when circumstances propose the right time. The site vacated is not abandoned, since structural elements of the hypermodules would be relandscaped to fill a new need. Predominant elements remaining on site would gain new significance in their old homes in the "Roman way." Rome recycled itself endlessly, and now in the process of the nth recycling Rome is quite an enchanting folly of old and new.

The most promising effect of the lean urban ribbon is a network of logistically distributed habitats capable, in time, of cleansing the land by substantially reducing an enormous fossil-fuel dependence, thus restoring ecosystems and enriching the life of the countryside now under the threat of endless sprawl. The lean urban ribbon would connect large and small existing habitats and help salvage the land from diaspora, while in a sustainable fashion reducing waste, pollution, and social and cultural impoverishment. In addition, each module of Lean Linear could define its special distinguishing characteristics: products, facilities, ethnicities, health practices, technologies, fashion, cuisine, and conviviality aligned sequentially along regional and continental routes.

Circumstances on a crowding planet are demanding urban systems of all sizes and originality that coordinate into continental hyperorganisms, producing a homospherical network of Lean Linear arterial cities. Time to get planners and architects to ponder their responsibilities in comprehensively reformulating the landscape. The moment is unequaled in view of the transformative power of the productive and marketing avalanches that *Homo faber* is generating.

Lean Linear City module variations

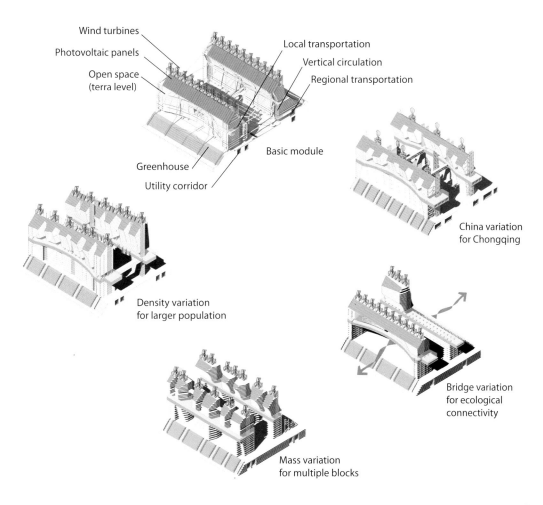

Wind turbines

Photovoltaic panels

Open space
(terra level)

Local transportation

Vertical circulation

Regional transportation

Basic module

Greenhouse

Utility corridor

China variation
for Chongqing

Density variation
for larger population

Bridge variation
for ecological
connectivity

Mass variation
for multiple blocks

Module components and floor plans

Level 0   Level 1   Level 3

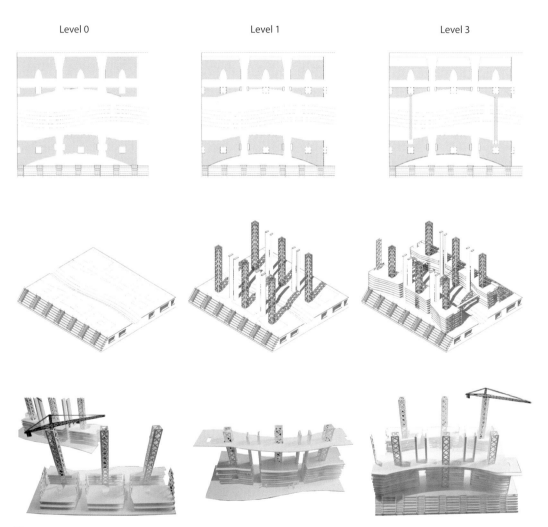

Level 10   Level 20   Level 23

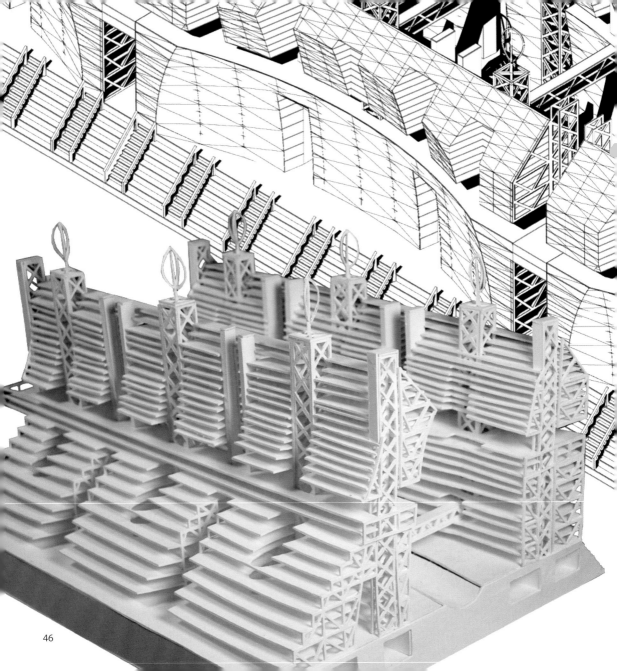

47

Lean Linear City module section

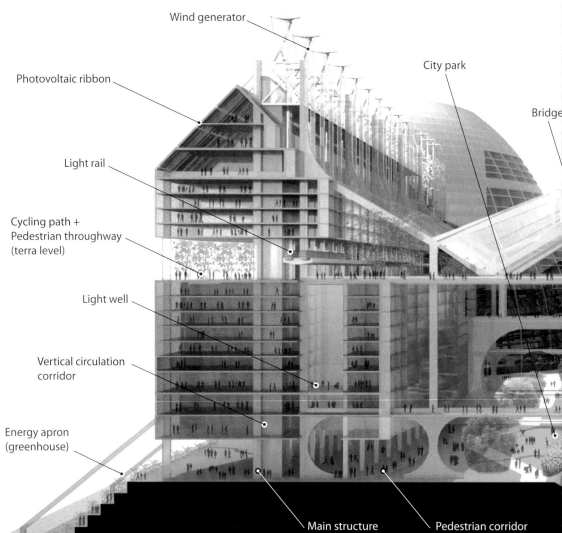

Wind generator

City park

Photovoltaic ribbon

Bridge

Light rail

Cycling path +
Pedestrian throughway
(terra level)

Light well

Vertical circulation
corridor

Energy apron
(greenhouse)

Main structure

Pedestrian corridor

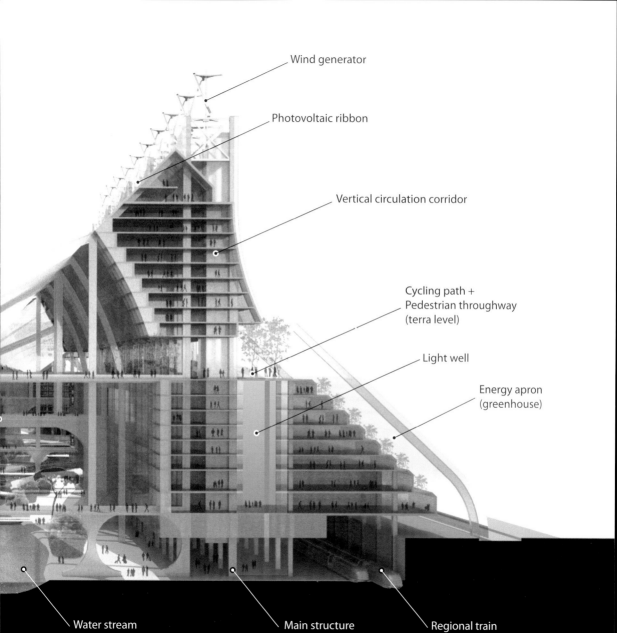

Wind generator

Photovoltaic ribbon

Vertical circulation corridor

Cycling path +
Pedestrian throughway
(terra level)

Light well

Energy apron
(greenhouse)

Water stream

Main structure

Regional train

Logistical network integrating the urban nodes and modules

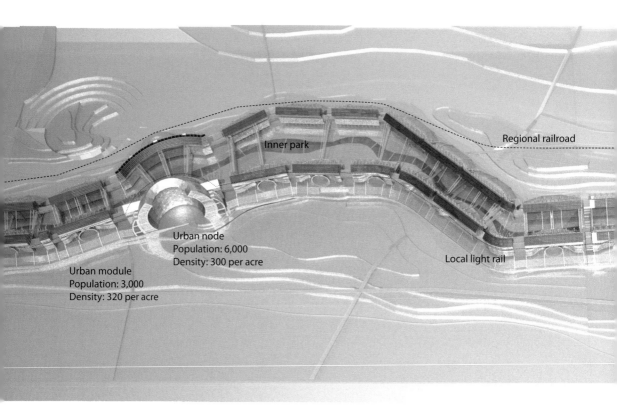

Regional railroad

Inner park

Urban node
Population: 6,000
Density: 300 per acre

Local light rail

Urban module
Population: 3,000
Density: 320 per acre

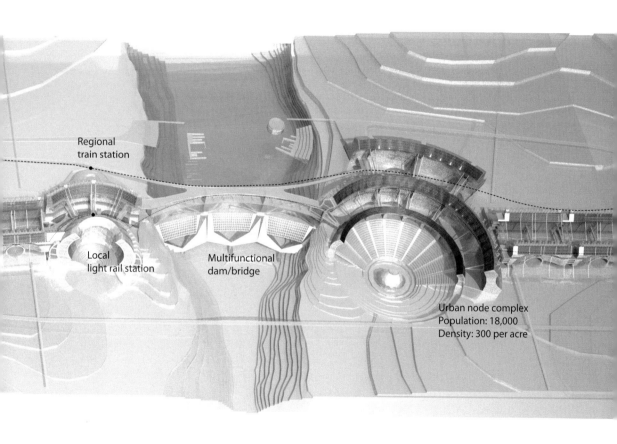

Regional
train station

Local
light rail station

Multifunctional
dam/bridge

Urban node complex
Population: 18,000
Density: 300 per acre

55

Logistics

Lean Linear City is based on three major transportation modes: pedestrian walkways, cycling paths, and mass-transit and vertical-transport systems. The linear nature of the urban-ribbon structure is meant to follow the urban logistical system, connecting different cultural interests and economic needs both horizontally and linearly. Lean Linear also has high enough density to justify a multilevel, public circulation system. Public accessibility at multiple levels encourages walking, cycling, and the use of other low-impact transport mechanisms. Sustainable mobility should address the problem of energy inefficiency and pollution caused by conventional logistical systems while creating a healthier lifestyle for residents.

Pedestrian, bicycle, local light rail
Pedestrian, bicycle corridor
Pedestrian, bicycle parkway
Regional train

Pedestrian inner park with water stream

Pedestrian throughway, cycling path, and local light rail

Terra-level pedestrian park space

Energy

Depending on regional climatic and topographical conditions, Lean Linear introduces alternative energy production options: continuous arrays of photovoltaic modules harvesting solar energy and series of windmills capturing wind energy. Both systems are located at the top of the structures, taking advantage of nonpolluting renewable energy. Passive solar features such as glazed park spaces and attached greenhouses (the energy apron) add to the energy efficiency of the building. If all combinations of the suggested energy production and efficiency systems were employed for the urban modules, they would support 50–80 percent of the modules' energy needs.

Photovoltaic panels
Wind turbines
Greenhouse
Inner park space

Solar-panel roofs as an energy source for the city

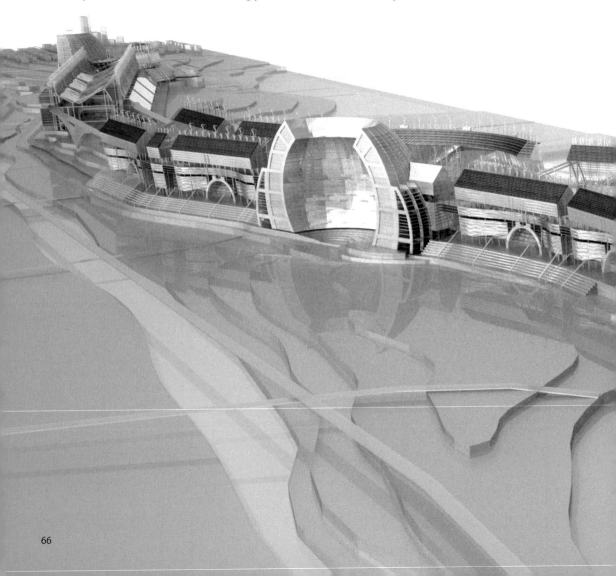

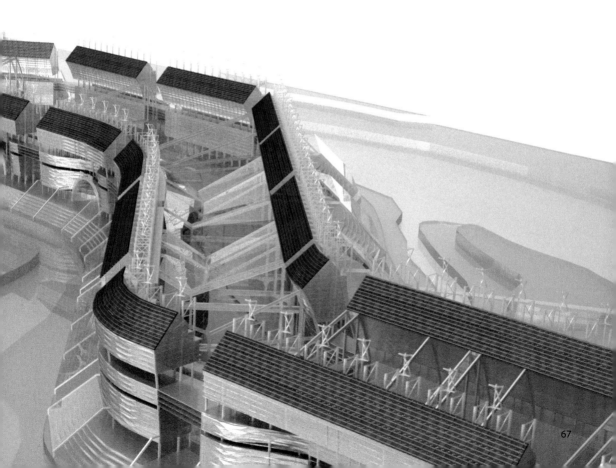

Wind turbines augmenting local energy needs

Urban park space enabling a passive energy strategy

Agriculture

Lean Linear's attempt to reduce food mileage, which piles up energy and environmental costs, necessitates bringing agricultural activities much closer to the habitat where the consumption occurs. Lean Linear explores urban agriculture in the adjacent open fields and vertical farms built into the structure where applicable. Another feature of Lean Linear is the terraced greenhouse unit, intended to extend the growing season and provide diversified horticulture and floriculture practices within its stratified microclimatic conditions. This glazed environment substantially reduces the quantity of water used while diverting excess heat to upper structures for space heating when needed.

Greenhouse energy apron
Orchard apron

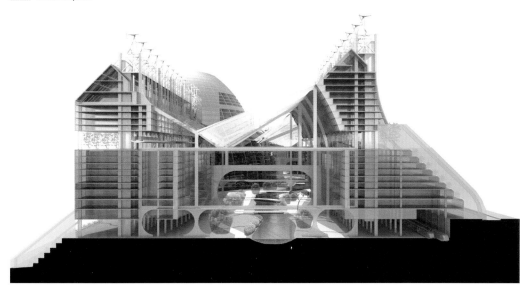

Greenhouse for urban agriculture and heat-energy production

Orchard apron providing local agriculture

ARCOLOGY 5-D/4'5

Lean Linear City model for China, 11m x 1.5m, scale = 1:1000

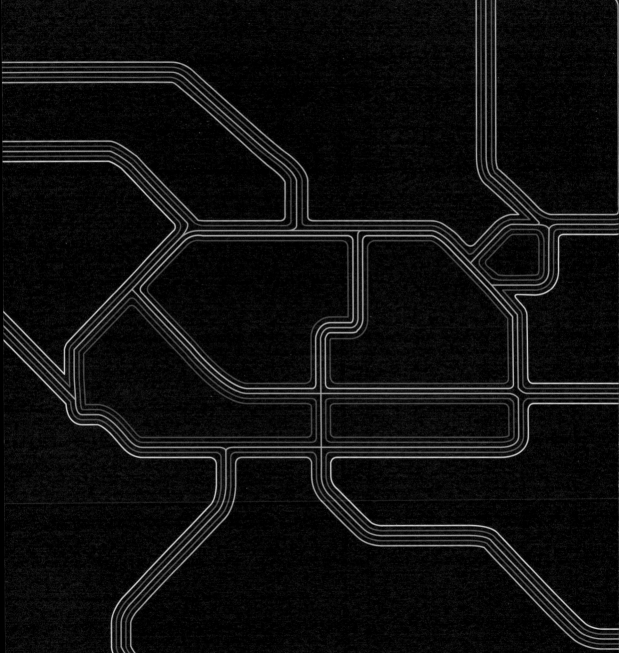

Lean Alternative

The lean credo is: "Do more with less." The lean habitat lessens dependence on massive injections of appliances, furnishings, equipment, gadgetries, and the enchantment of buying for the sake of buying, while two billion people are deprived of food, shelter, and dignity. Squalor does not just imply an impoverished, dilapidated physical place. Squalor resides also in the most opulent environs.

Squalor resides where human dignity is trashed. Whereas we work assiduously to solve technical dysfunction when it occurs, we too easily go along with ethical dysfunction. Even when the dysfunction is out of ignorance, this does not excuse the specific case, but merely obfuscates its causes.

Lean society could be lethal for greed and materialism by decontaminating individuals and groups of people. Decontamination fights the overstuffing that has besieged our environments and minds.

Nature squanders activity, achieving one success among a thousand failures. But for each successful species, what triumphs is frugality. Coral reefs, Amazonian forests, termite "cities," worm societies, wildebeest herds, and human settlements are all lean living communities. They survive, reproduce, and prosper on a hyperlean diet of sunlight and spare minerals (including water). The whole process of the cosmos's interiorization—the mineral kingdom becoming self-conscious—is an éclat of the potency and potential of leanness. This is what I call the "lean alternative," a cause for endless celebration.

Saguaro National Park,
Tucson, Arizona, USA, 2009

It is not right to say that the city is like an organism, but it is perhaps more telling and normatively useful to say that the city is a hyperorganism; that is to say it has to find whatever accommodation it might desire not in letting go of self-control and self-discipline but introducing them in their self-transcending dimension. Mankind, designed for thousands of generations by the planetary environment, is now more and more designing its own immediate environment. This makes architecture a cultural-societal keystone, and history testifies to this.

Manhattan,
New York City, USA, 2009

Organisms are lean phenomena. Once conceived, they do so much with so little. The lean alternative is an attempt to reformulate the materialistic tide into a considered balance, where production, consumption, and worth form a balancing act, a graceful trinity working on the basis and inspiration of knowledge, learning, and transcendence.

Suncheon coastal wetland,
Jeonnam, Korea, 2008

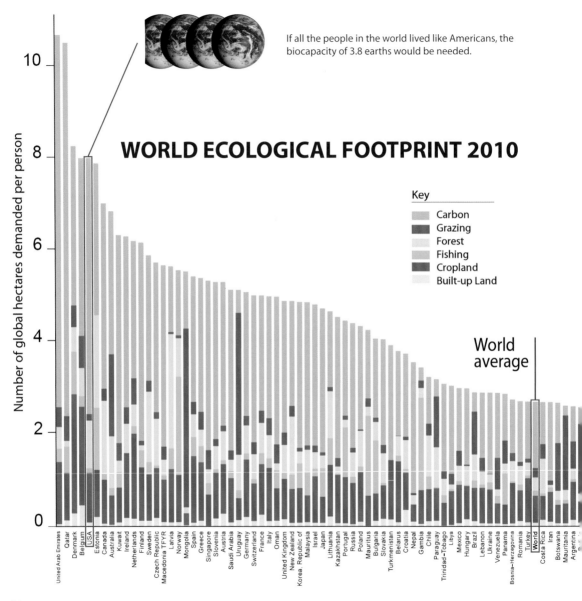

WORLD ECOLOGICAL FOOTPRINT 2010

If all the people in the world lived like Americans, the biocapacity of 3.8 earths would be needed.

Number of global hectares demanded per person (y-axis, 0–10)

Key
- Carbon
- Grazing
- Forest
- Fishing
- Cropland
- Built-up Land

World average

Countries (x-axis, left to right): United Arab Emirates, Qatar, Denmark, Belgium, USA, Estonia, Canada, Australia, Kuwait, Ireland, Netherlands, Finland, Sweden, Czech Republic, Macedonia TFYR, Latvia, Norway, Mongolia, Spain, Greece, Singapore, Slovenia, Austria, Saudi Arabia, Uruguay, Germany, Switzerland, France, Italy, Oman, United Kingdom, New Zealand, Korea, Republic of, Malaysia, Israel, Japan, Lithuania, Kazakhstan, Portugal, Russia, Poland, Mauritius, Bulgaria, Slovakia, Belarus, Croatia, Nepal, Gambia, Chile, Paraguay, Trinidad-Tobago, Libya, Mexico, Hungary, Brazil, Lebanon, Ukraine, Venezuela, Panama, Bosnia-Herzegovina, Romania, Turkey, World, Costa Rica, Iran, Botswana, Mauritania, Argentina

Given the size of the projected global population, ten billion or so people, the carrying capacity of the biosphere, and the dereliction afflicting more than half of the human population, the hyperconsumptive frenzy seems ungainly and unrealistic. It might also turn out to be detrimental to the aim of transcendence that *Homo sapiens* is and ought to be engaged in.

Whatever we use and dump has a multiplier attached, from the seven-billion multiplier in the toilet paper domain (consuming a little forest), to computers, with *x* million users per unit (all too soon on its way to the dump), and so on. This would help us get a sense of connection and belonging as well as a sense of our burgeoning and multiplying dumpsites.

Since three friends of mine used up a roll of toilet paper in two days, I readily extrapolate: the forest that we seven billion people flush down the toilet could be cut by half, a third, or a fourth: hundreds of square kilometers of actual living, growing forest salvaged through a collective moment of concern. The frugal life! Extrapolations of this kind in the office and elsewhere may help put our actions into real context and give us better awareness of what an impact trivial consumption can have on whole cultures and the biosphere.

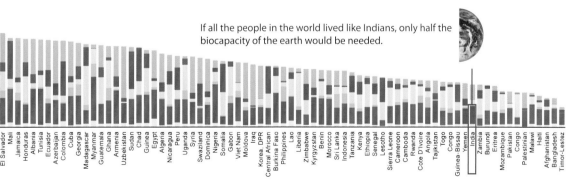

If all the people in the world lived like Indians, only half the biocapacity of the earth would be needed.

Source: Living Planet Report 2010, Biodiversity, biocapacity and development, 2010, World Wildlife Fund

Though we are approaching the threshold of being able to provide food, shelter, and education for all people, we are immensely far from achieving anything like universal equity in distribution of such resources.

The lean alternative is not local, regional, or national in scope; it responds to a transnational need faced by rich and poor nations alike. It is instrumental because it advocates the pursuit of equity by establishing a habitat that encourages coherence with the most valuable inclination of our species: the optimization of mind via the optimization of our presence on the planet.

Any nonlean approach would be a planetary curse if extended to a projected ten billion people. This is not abstract thinking. This is hardcore realism for a human phenomenon that has not yet found a realistic response to the logistic-based nature of its species's development.

Lean society is a realistic proposition that could embrace have and have-not alike. It is evolutionarily more coherent than the hyperconsumption society. Evolution might well be poised for an unparalleled acceleration, courtesy of learning and doing's new technologies.

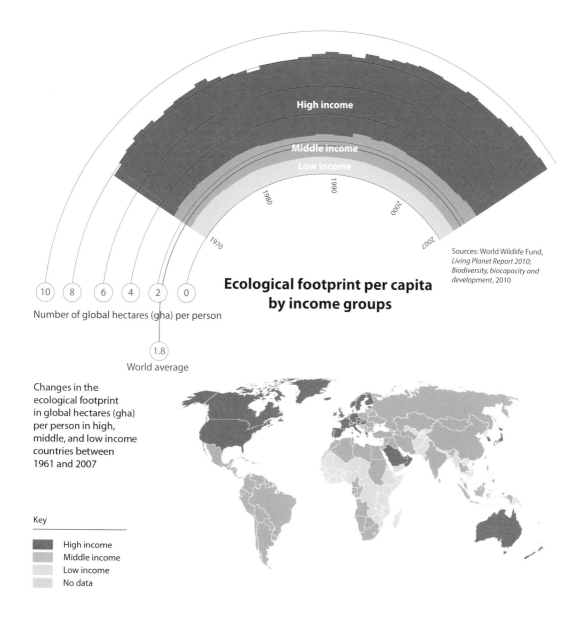

Ecological footprint per capita by income groups

High income

Middle income

Low income

1980 1990 2000 2007 1970

10 8 6 4 2 0

Number of global hectares (gha) per person

1.8

World average

Sources: World Wildlife Fund, *Living Planet Report 2010*; *Biodiversity, biocapacity and development*, 2010

Changes in the ecological footprint in global hectares (gha) per person in high, middle, and low income countries between 1961 and 2007

Key

High income
Middle income
Low income
No data

Leanness is agile, mercurial, sensitized, and alert about the ever-precarious condition of people that gets buried in materialism's obesity. For this reason, the lean-alternative imperative is as significant in consumerist countries as it is in have-not countries. In consumerist countries, the lean alternative needs to abate consumerist aggression. The planet at large would be the winner.

Highline,
New York City, USA, 2010

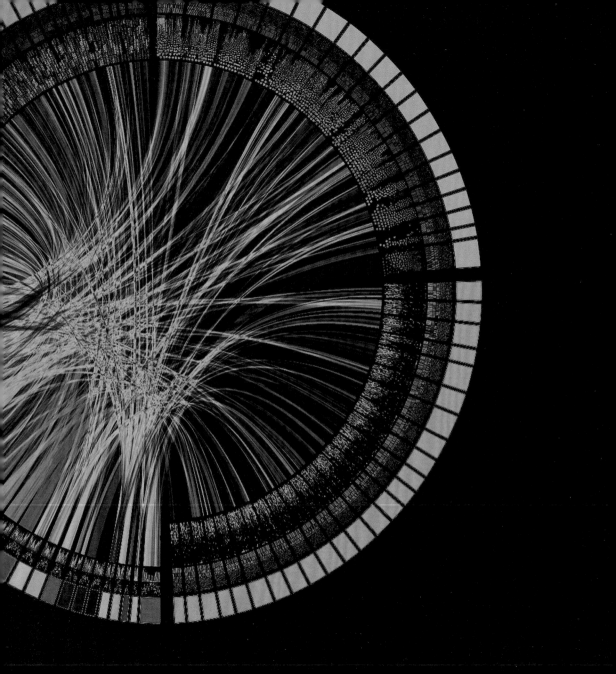

Miniaturization-Complexity

Life on this planet originates and evolves courtesy of complexity and miniaturization that combine in a critical mass of such intensity that volition and "religion" (bonding) are triggered within the cellular envelopes we call organisms. I call this stupendous and stupefying event the "urban effect." Evolution testifies to the indispensability and power of the urban effect. The urban effect is, then, proposed as the recurring and imperative effect running through evolution from the very early unicellular organism onward, and it is characterized with ever growing force by the implosion of a relatively indifferent milieu, the nonliving universe, into discrete, discriminately complex, and necessarily miniaturized systems.

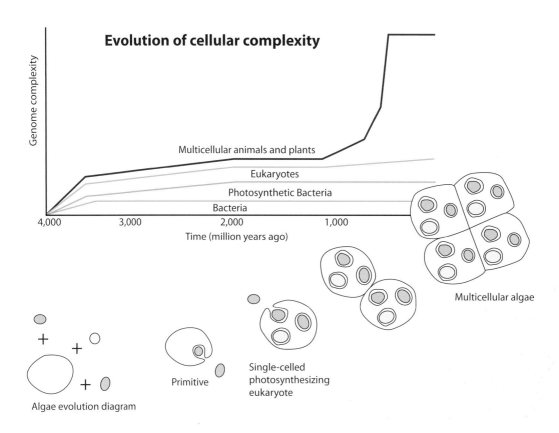

Evolution of cellular complexity

Genome complexity

Multicellular animals and plants

Eukaryotes

Photosynthetic Bacteria

Bacteria

4,000   3,000   2,000   1,000

Time (million years ago)

Multicellular algae

Single-celled photosynthesizing eukaryote

Primitive

Algae evolution diagram

This process of complexification is labeled "urban effect" because the city is the system, more than any other, that sees the transition of the already unbelievable complexity of the human phenomenon into even more improbable occasions: the political, economic, social, ethical, cultural, scientific, esthetic, and technological totality, which is more than the sum of all its parts and is the epitome of complexity. The coherence of the process through which the cell becomes the city is based on the exponential accretion of complexity by which information becomes knowledge and knowledge becomes the new mover for creation.

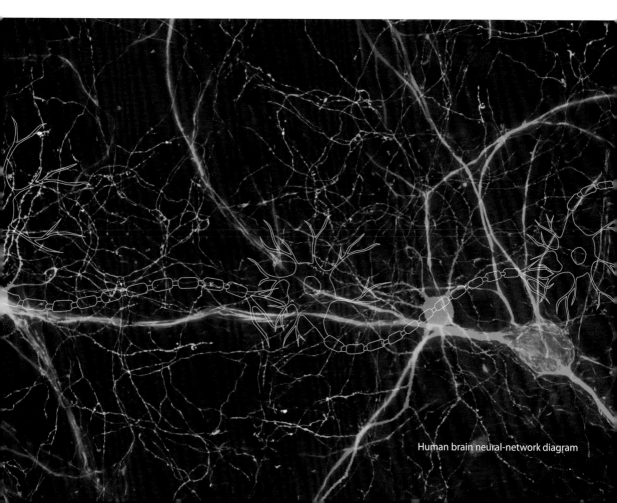

Human brain neural-network diagram

A continent dotted with myriad "peaceful, nature-loving" suburban villages works against the drift of conscious life since the Industrial Revolution toward increasing complexity, the very complexity that generates the true urban context with its inimitable richness. Life, as nature tells us, is in the thick of things: this pertains to organisms of the biosphere as well as the hyperorganism constituted by the lives and activities of towns and cities.

Rio Duoro, Porto, Portugal, 2006

Complexity is a worthwhile goal in planning and building cities because organisms at all levels of evolution are masterworks of complexity indissolubly tied to miniaturization. A society made up of complex individuals is a society defining ever more intricate synergies, as we all know when surveying our lives.

Complexity: The complex is not the complicated or the confusing, but a group of interrelated activities or ideas that form a single coherent whole. Wherever a living process goes on, many events and processes cluster. These processes are immensely complex and the effects are ever intensifying.

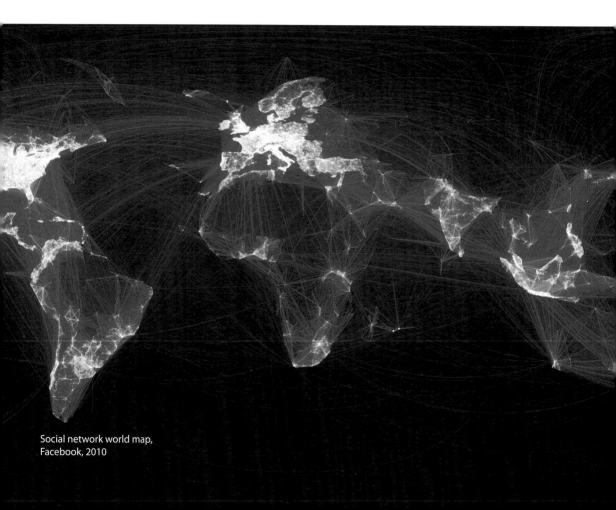

Social network world map, Facebook, 2010

Miniaturization: The nature of complexity demands the rigorous utilization of all resources: mass-energy and space-time, for example. Therefore, wherever complexity is at work, miniaturization is mandated as part of the process. The miniaturized is not the congested or the gridlocked, but that which is made small and compact by means of efficient organization.

Rackmount server: Aberdeen Stirling S15 Dual Xeon. Motherboard: Supermicro P4DPR-6GM+

For a long time we have been aware (unconsciously perhaps) of the critical nature of complexity ("I am complex, ergo I become") and perhaps even aware of the importance of reducing the space and time required—via miniaturization—for the timely and effective transformation of our world. (Cities are emblematic of such necessity, as products of the "urban effect"). Whenever we leave a system we have been working on, such system had better be more complex (i.e., richer, more capable) than it was when we entered it.

The degree of complexity in and of the organic (carbon cycle) is for the moment immensely greater than in the inorganic (silicon cycle). Billions of years of exertion in self-creation remain an unequaled experience to date. With respect to miniaturization, silicon is for now a pale emulator of its formidable parental premises (carbon). In addition, it is an instrumentality in search of context that probably only the grace of passion can deliver. The elegant instrument (silicon domain) is not yet capable of esthetic transcendence. The first logical machine serenading whatever, will be the threshold into a new grace. Will it be able to do that nonpassionately?

Miniaturization is the password of the day. Miniaturization speaks of space, occupancy, bulk, incumbency, three dimensionality, diminution; they all speak of geometry; they speak of becoming reality as space in metamorphosis. Geometry, geometry, geometry… The pulse of geometry as self-creating reality: the lean (minimalist) hypothesis. The "miracles" reality seems to be performing "effortlessly, routinely" here and there in its own space immensity are coming about in the nanogeometry and nanobiogeometry of its metamorphosing. A furious metamorphosing trillions of pulses per second, a speed we cannot begin to grasp since we are made by it—the *mysterium tremendum*.

iPad, 2011

ENIAC, 1946

Arcology

Nudging Space Arcology

My work as an architect-planner under the influence of the lean alternative has proposed the development of urban systems I have called arcologies. I developed the notion of arcology (architecture + ecology) in the 1950s and 1960s. The name arcology indicates that architecture and ecology should work in tandem. These are lean three-dimensional structures analogous to the structures of organisms and hyperorganisms. A self-sustaining "confederation" of organisms, such as those of termites, ants, bees, are successful protoconsciousness systems, deprived of the self-creative élan of cities. Both unaware insect "cities" and human cities are codified by similar rules: bonding (*religare*) and intent (volition).

The arcology concept proposes a highly integrated and compact three-dimensional urban form that pursues the opposite of urban sprawl, with its inherently wasteful consumption of land, energy, and time, tending to isolate people from each other and community life. In an arcology, the built environment and the living processes of the inhabitants interact as organs, tissues, and cells do in a highly evolved organism. This means that multiple systems work together, coordinated and integrated to minimize waste while maximizing efficient circulation of people and resources, employing multi-use structures, and exploiting solar orientation for lighting, heating, cooling, food production, and esthetic impact.

ARCHITECTURE + ECOLOGY

Arcosanti, Arizona,
USA, 2005

The essential problem I am confronting is the present design of cities only a few stories high, stretching outward in unwieldy sprawl for kilometers. As a result of their sprawl, they literally transform the earth, turning farmland into parking lots and wasting enormous amounts of time and energy transporting people, goods, and services over their expanses. My proposition is urban implosion rather than explosion. The city must cohere with the guidelines of the evolution of life. These are self-containment, sophisticated logistics, reduction of waste (the lean process), interaction with the "outer" world, richness of processes, self-reliance, and the generation of an inner light, the urban persona.

The morphology of the tree, namely the proximity of the leaves to the logistical network of the branches, is an analogy for the swiftness and economy that our systems try to emulate to no avail. In the lean construct of an organism, each cell of the body is fed and cleansed by astounding reciprocal networks of arteries and veins. Trillions of cells are kept living and working by the gossamer reticulum of an inimitable delivery–retrieval system. Our monstrous multitudes of automobiles, soon over six billion (in accord with the American dream), will never achieve even a pale approximation of the logistical perfection of any organism. Furthermore, a culture based on the automobile leads to the diaspora of habitat, inevitably segregating people and stifling true novelty, the synergies of culture and civilization.

Novanoah1,
Soleri
arcology
design,
1969

Tree
circulation
diagram

121

In an organism, astronomical numbers become hyper-astronomical. In those "conditions," order and self-control (discipline) are mandatory. Without them, life is terminated instantaneously. What goes for persona goes for the hyper-persona, the city. If and when this critical state appears, the culture of a society produces civilization, the geometries of space become graceful: the esthetic. There are analogies between the working of an organism and the working of an "organization" like the city.

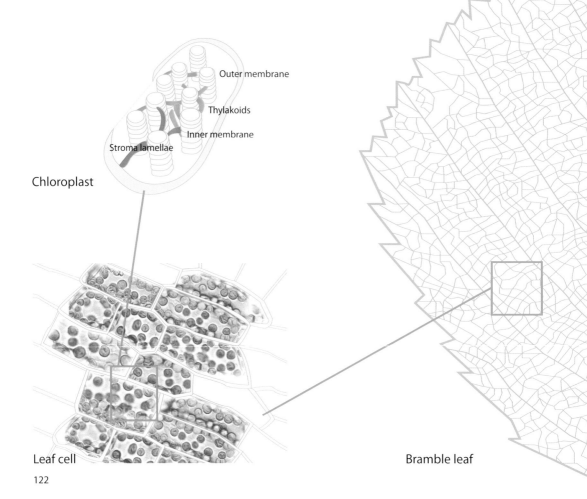

Outer membrane

Thylakoids

Inner membrane

Stroma lamellae

Chloroplast

Leaf cell

Bramble leaf

One that comes to mind is that in both there is division and specialization of labor and the tasks inherent to the responsibility of the participant. To make it short, a cell in an organism is assigned a task. One is assigned to the "rectal division," another to the "brain division." The magic is that there does not seem to be a conflict. All the zillions of cells working simultaneously and at closest distance are co-creators of the animal.

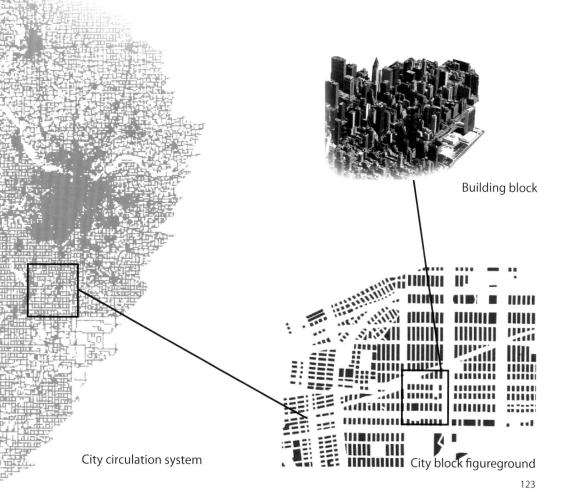

Building block

City circulation system

City block figureground

In the open fields we cultivate food for the organism; in the city we cultivate food for the persona, evidently not a black-and-white distinction but a distinction nevertheless. Since those cultural industries coexist, it is imperative to cultivate their synergy and develop a Culture, capital "c," that works at its own growth, the infinite mosaic of personal growth. It has taken and is taking a Promethean effort to shape the materialistic platform of capitalism under the "law of the jungle" (not the innocent rule of justness typifying the vegetal and animal survival rationale!). It would probably take no less of a Promethean effort to reach the postmaterialistic platform, giving us the platform of hyperjustness, the loving-esthetic platform.

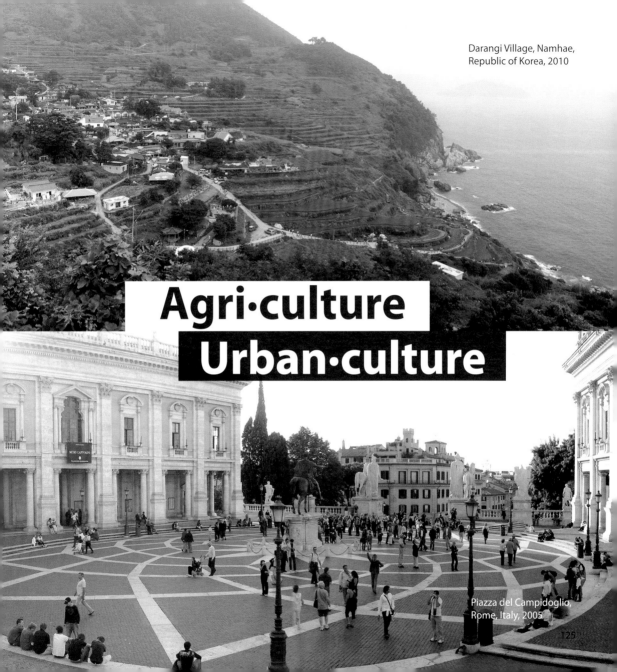

Darangi Village, Namhae, Republic of Korea, 2010

Agri·culture
Urban·culture

Piazza del Campidoglio, Rome, Italy, 2005

125

Italian Night,
Arcosanti, Arizona,
USA, 2010

A green city, an ecological city, would consist of residents who recognize that the urban phenomenon is the core of *humanitas*. A city implies the presence of a culture and the making of civilization.

Piazza del Campo, Siena, Italy, 2005

The wisest and most prudent architects and planners point to the city not as an organism but as a potpourri of one kind or another. Their fault might lie in ignoring the makeup of organisms, their genesis, and their possible transcendence into hyperorganism—the one composed of a thousand or a million body-brains—the city. The termite hill is a non-self-aware hyperorganism. The city is, or could be, a self-aware hyperorganism. An immense difference. The hyperorganism of the city is analogous to the body organism. But each of the billions of cell-personae wants to be "king of the castle." Where can an acceptable resolution be attempted? Hierarchy, excellence, vicariousness, generosity, leanness, "transcendence" (self-creation)—and a knowledge so profound as to be the spark of wisdom. Here, we are face to face with love. We experience intimations of it, so that notwithstanding the chaos-entropy, we carry on. The paramount priority? Knowledge-passion. Passionate knowing? You, I, and the garbage collector are one: *Homo sapiens* co-creating the "urban effect" analogous to organism.

Habitat is crucial in an age when the western societies of the "haves" seem to be bent on monopolizing land, resources, and culture at the expense of a more just and less materialistic inclination. This industry should occupy a large portion of society's activities, since habitat is central to our presence and our evolution on planet Earth. It should take precedence over all other occupations because of its impact on the biosphere and on the culture of all societies. For a project initiated in order to explore an alternative to the runaway train of hyperconsumption, any deviation from the task is betrayal, pure and simple. Even modest pioneering toward leanness is critical to the production that the human condition is most dependent on.

Average size of a new American
single-family house

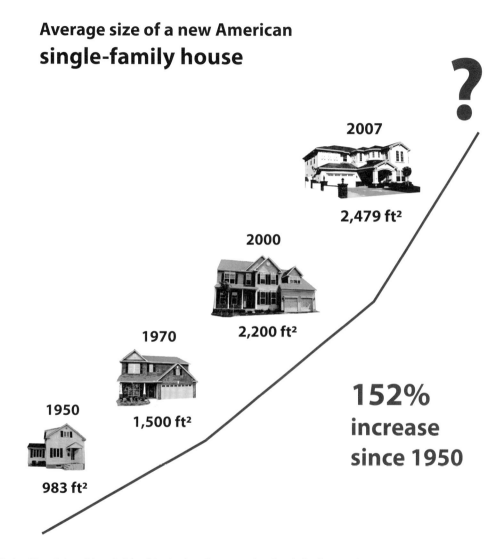

?

2007

2,479 ft²

2000

2,200 ft²

1970

1,500 ft²

1950

983 ft²

152%
increase
since 1950

National Association of Home Builders, "Housing facts, figures, trends and single-family square footage by location," 2007;
U.S. Census Bureau, A. Wilson, and J. Boehland, "Small is beautiful, U.S. house size, resource use, and the environment," 2005.

One of the distinguishing features of humankind is its potential and power to transform things. *Homo faber*, through the inception of science and technology, has become the epitome of howness: how anything can practically be made into something else. The recent few centuries, but mainly the recent few generations with their billions of people, have begun to transform the living skin of the planet in critical ways, and now even the cosmos at large might be affected. This howness onslaught is dramatically changing most of our cultures. In fact we have to reformulate the nexus of individual and society, man and nature, man and the imponderable. Given our skill as transformers, as *Homo faber*, the evolutionary tide has been literally taking us to the edge of catastrophe. The materialism we have been cultivating is part of our evolutionary history, and its explosion on the historical stage is due to the productivity of technocracy. We are cursed by the capriciousness of *Homo faber*, inebriated by breakneck technological capabilities. We have invented a virtual reality, a whole new world voraciously hungry for its own tools and toys.

The hyperconsumption now charming nations does not call forcefully enough for the coherence and idealism now necessary to prevent *Homo faber* suicide. Since production-consumption thrives on gigantism, I think the wisest initiative for all environmental concerns is the drastic reduction of consumption (oil consumption the icon of them all). This entails reformulating the character of human habitat in the direction of a return to urban culture-civilization, historically proven (over some 10,000 years?) to be coherent with how all of life sustains itself.

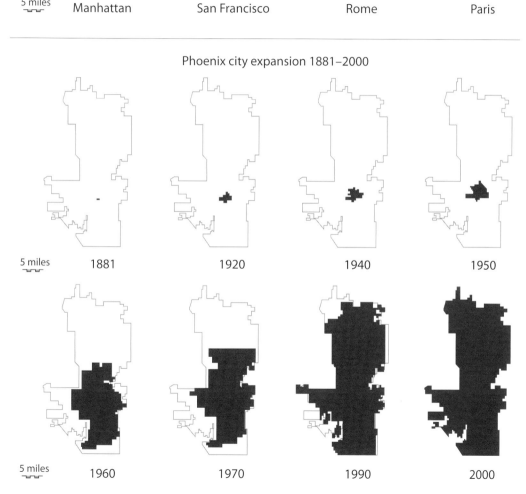

5 miles

Manhattan   San Francisco   Rome   Paris

Phoenix city expansion 1881–2000

5 miles

1881   1920   1940   1950

5 miles

1960   1970   1990   2000

Credit: Ignacio San Martin, Phoenix city expansion and area comparison study, 2000

We live in a critical moment when *Homo faber* is engaged in a lopsided action for the privileged half of seven billion people, while one third of us, all persons by the way, is in the midst of misery. It ought to be indispensable, imperative, that architects and planners would be concerned with the state of towns and cities historically engaged in "cultivating" the culture and civilization that I call the urban effect. Since the volume of humanity in search of fulfillment is now immense, seven billion of us (plus the pet biomass), we no longer have the luxury of doing what pleases us as personas because doing "what pleases me" is seldom imbued with the knowledge and wisdom indispensable to satisfy "the needs of us."

Organisms are not privatized phenomena. They are highly synergetic bundles of volition and *religare*. The hyperorganism of culture and civilization is not flat exurbia, but the tridimensional city, where space is utilized as a precious resource. The "religious" aspect of space, with its quickening pace of self-generating geometries, is the basis of the urban landscape. The preeminence of the city, definer of civilization, is now even more indispensable given the trend toward materialism advocated by millions, transfixed by the American dream, which is now spawning all the techno-plutocratic-obese opportunistic frenzy that human ingenuity and rapaciousness can generate.

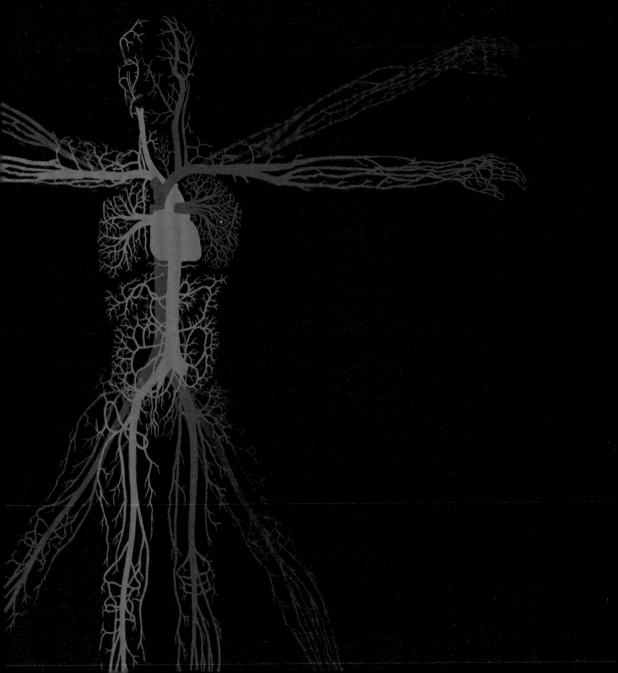

Arterial Arcology

What is needed is a total REFORMULATION.

– Paolo Soleri

Lean Linear City as an Arterial Arcology

Tomiaki Tamura

> *City planning is not discovery, not invention, not a corporate enterprise, not big business, although in it all of this is present. Unless it is a creative act embodying, while unfolding substance and longing, a conceiving the physical shell for man's endeavors, individual and social, it will a priori degrade any potentiality to a mere technical meeting of needs, and to a gilded cage for survival.* —The Sketchbooks of Paolo Soleri (1970)

These words were written when Soleri embarked on his first major urban project, Mesa City, in 1960. The proposal placed a city 10 kilometers wide and 35 kilometers long on a hypothetical mesa, an iconic topography of the American southwest. The city was designed for two million inhabitants.

As reflected in the design vocabulary used in Soleri's latest project, Lean Linear City, Mesa City featured the three-dimensionally organized urban complexes that encourage multifunctional activities within its proximity. These activities employed renewable energy applications and water-waste management systems, while balancing natural and man-made environments.

Soleri's penetrating insights into city planning through the Mesa City design exercise went beyond simply providing technical solutions for sustainable urban development. He took aesthetic and equity considerations as desirable and indispensable elements for maintaining a healthy environment. Soleri also pointed out the pitfalls often present in our technocratic and profit-driven society. He went on to suggest the need for "creative acts" and "compassion" to fully explore human potential in his endeavor on paper.

Interestingly, Mesa City featured multi-bands of urban transit systems integrating city amenities and habitats. The logistical loops included a mass-transit system, a waterway, and even a highway with limited use of automobiles, all becoming part of the city's vertebrae. Thus Soleri's first version of a linear city was born. Mesa City's design parameters became the precursory guidelines for arcology, Soleri's more radicalized and comprehensive urban theory, developed a decade later.

Around the same period, architect Konstantinos Doxiadis observed the growth patterns of major cities around the world in his book *Ekistic* (1968) and predicted the inevitable amalgamation of megalopolises, forming what he called Ecumenopolis, a global city that consists of a continuous mass of human habitats. Soleri also recognized such a trend, but characterized it as "The Map of Despair" in his book, *Arcology: The City in the Image of Man* (1969), which presented suggestions for a more positive potential scenario for the future—in the spirit of what could be, instead of what is.

David Owen writes, in *Green Metropolis* (2009), about the values of dense cities functioning with public transportation systems and providing accessibility to cultural and commercial activities. Owen argues that New York City, Hong Kong, and other dense cities, although far from perfect, are more ecological than many of the so-called eco-conscious developments popping up worldwide. This becomes self-evident when energy consumption per capita and measurements of quality of life are taken into consideration. His observation resonates with the core notion of Soleri's arcology: a pedestrian-based community enhanced by public transportation systems to foster urban mobility. This in turn provides accessibility to urban amenities and the surrounding environment within a 24/7 mixed-use continuum, which enhances what Soleri calls the urban effect.

Arcology theory suggests a more holistic and interdisciplinary approach to address many complex urban issues. Modernization brought society the pursuit of efficiency and high productivity through specializations in practically every field. Globalization of commerce is an example. Entities that can deliver goods more efficiently and economically, regardless of environmental and human impact, get the competitive edge. Society has lost the holistic (macro) perspective in the process.

In the past century the development of hydrocarbon technology and our need for urban mobility gave us the automobile. Initially the automobile was an object of desire, then it became a necessity, now it is the cause of urban paralysis—especially as emerging economic powers have come to share the prosperity of the West. Even advanced clean-automobile technology cannot offset the ever more wasteful infrastructure supporting its logistical needs.

Soleri does not negate the technology of the automobile systematically. What he criticizes is unbridled dependence on the automobile that allows it to dominate the urban landscape. The result is endless urban sprawl contributing to the destruction of the environment. Soleri, therefore, insists on the "reformulation" of our urban-planning strategies.

The driving engine for reformulation, according to Soleri, is the lean alternative, which is a frugal and elegant commitment to induce a more equitable and sustainable development of human experience. It calls for a radical restructuring of our built environment to provide the inhabitants shared and fair access to city's activities, thereby establishing elements of equity while promoting quality of life in a sustainable manner. This alternative is presented through Soleri's Lean Linear City arterial arcology. It suggests a new socio-cultural-economic model by reconfiguring urban topography to achieve a robust and efficient cultural continuum.

In my opinion, while carbon neutrality is within reach through innovations in building technology and alternative-energy applications, the most important contribution of Lean Linear City is the logistical approach to defining and controlling growth patterns of existing and future cities. Furthermore, it can play a complimentary role to remedy existing cities in need of urban growth and redevelopment, while benefiting from vital access to existing metropolitan jobs and services that Lean Linear City may initially lack. As Lean Linear City grows, it can become an integral part of future urban nodes built along a cosmopolitan axis. Support activities along the arterial path include strategically placed energy-production systems, food supply, habitats for living and working, and other systems that become part of what Soleri calls "neo-nature."

The question becomes, if not now, when? Humanity faces overwhelming challenges: man-made and natural disasters, climate change, population growth, health implications, energy and material consumption, and so on. The implementation of a plan like Lean Linear City is not easy, if not impossible. There are many issues to be resolved for the project to be viable; logistical planning, construction costs, property acquisition (eminent domain), job access, economic development, ecological impact, technological research, and the list goes on. While acknowledging that no

plan can accommodate everyone, a small fraction of our urban development opportunities can provide room for transformation. "Reformulation" can begin now.

Again, this passage from Soleri's notes on Mesa City, written a half century ago, still resonates with his current proposal of the Lean Linear City.

> *Now, under the pressure of the human biological flood and the complexification of life, a reverence for nature combined with a maturing consciousness of the aesthetic-compassionate nature of man and the skill and power of self-adjourning technology will transfigure the earth, and man will construct human ecologies . . . Webbed in the wilderness, in the agricultural expanses, and in the seas, powerfully built organisms, modular ecologies, would rise high in the sky, roots deep in land and seas.* —The Sketchbooks of Paolo Soleri (1970)

Density and Transportation Systems of Lean Linear City

Youngsoo Kim

Population density and logistical systems are two interrelated and synergetic factors that play a key role in the city—affecting every aspect from energy consumption to socioeconomic sustainability. The Lean Linear City proposal by Paolo Soleri and Arcosanti Planning Department employs high-density development following the mass-transit corridor as a means to maximize the synergetic effect of population density and logistical systems, while also minimizing fuel consumption, especially by private automobile use.

Destination proximity within the city, enabled by dense development, allows residents to reduce routine travel distances. This increases logistical efficiency while lessening fuel consumption for transportation. Dense development—that is, constructing higher and more compact buildings—decreases the footprint of the city, which simultaneously reduces energy use for their construction and maintenance. The logistical systems of Lean Linear mostly consist of pedestrian and cycling routes, public-transportation lines, and private automobile roadways. Well-planned connectivity between the mass-transit lines and the pedestrian and cycling routes reinforces even further the proximity effect that density brings to the city. Provided with more options for their mode of transportation, inhabitants of Lean Linear become less dependent on private vehicles and consume substantially less fuel per capita. This also enhances walkability and the quality of pedestrian experience in the city.

Here is a comparison of two cities shaped by obviously contrasting density and transportation systems: Amsterdam and Phoenix. Amsterdam, in northern Europe, is home to 780,000 people living within its city area of 219 square kilometers. It is one of the densest cities in the world at 3,500 people per square kilometer, with four metro lines and sixteen tram lines serving 260 million people per year. Phoenix, in Arizona, USA, is home to approximately 1.5 million people within an area of 1,341 square kilometers. It has twice the population and six times the geographic area of Amsterdam, resulting in one-third the population density by comparison, or 1,100 people per square kilometer. In 2008 Phoenix built a single light-rail metro line serving 15 million people annually, which is one-seventeenth the ridership served by Amsterdam's metro.

Amsterdam–Phoenix comparison

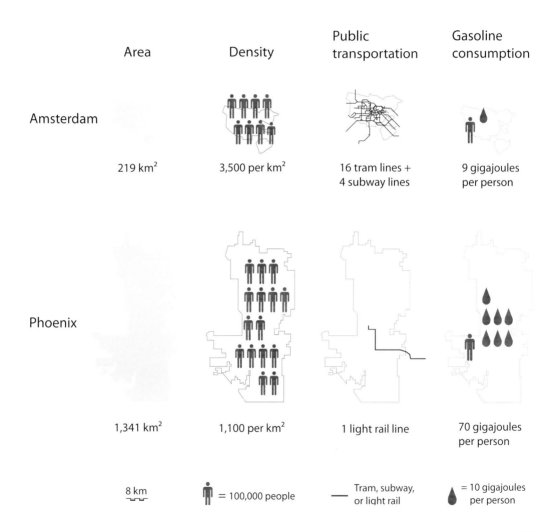

	Area	Density	Public transportation	Gasoline consumption
Amsterdam	219 km²	3,500 per km²	16 tram lines + 4 subway lines	9 gigajoules per person
Phoenix	1,341 km²	1,100 per km²	1 light rail line	70 gigajoules per person

8 km

👤 = 100,000 people

— Tram, subway, or light rail

💧 = 10 gigajoules per person

Phoenix has a 2.3 percent public-transportation use rate compared with a 25 percent use rate in Amsterdam. While 75 percent of inhabitants commute by car in Phoenix, only 35 percent in Amsterdam do (Buheler and Pucher, 2010; Artibise, Gammage Jr., Welch, 2008). This wide discrepancy is reflected in annual petroleum consumption per capita, which in Phoenix is seven times that of Amsterdam (Newman and Kenworthy, 1989).

These examples set forth two contrasting urban-development strategies: high density population served by a mass-transit system, on the one hand, and low density population highly dependent on a private-automobile system, on the other. Although both examples are situated in developed countries, they can serve as critical models for emerging economies, including that of China, as they confront environmentally and socially challenging rapid urbanization. For the last three decades, the urban population of China has grown about 281 percent, while that of the United States has grown 60 percent (UN World Urbanization Prospects, 2007). One of the main drivers of rapid urban growth is the migration trend from rural to urban areas. The rural-to-urban migration of 103 million people between 1990 and 2005 accounts for 32 percent of China's urban population growth. Urban expansion by agglomeration of adjacent land and natural population increase contributed about 40 percent of urban population growth in China (McKinsey Global Institute, 2009).

Chongqing was created in 1997 as one of four municipalities in China that are directly controlled by the national government (previously it was a sub-provincial city of Sichuan province). Both in terms of population and land area, it is the largest direct-controlled municipality in China, with 28 million inhabiting an area of 82,401 square kilometers. The area of Chongqing municipality is equivalent to that of the state of Alabama in the US. Since its establishment as a municipality, Chongqing has been the central hub of China's development campaign in its western regions (Chongqing Yearbook, 2009).

Chongqing is an informative case to study due to its unique spatial and demographic condition: it exemplifies urban growth caused by the rural-migration trend within its municipal area. On the macro scale, Chongqing consists of three major regions: the one-hour-drive circle in the western part and two wings in the eastern part of the municipality (see diagram at right). The former constitutes a more compact urban area, the latter a large rural area of Chongqing.

Chongqing demographic information

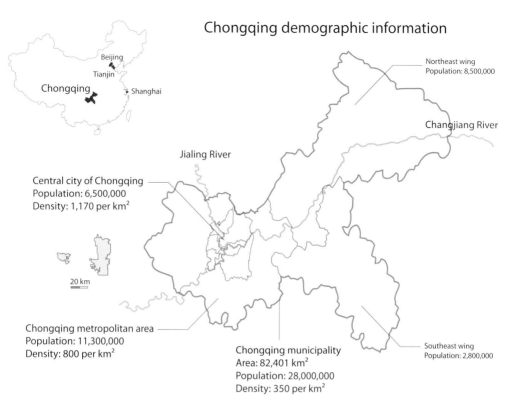

Beijing

Tianjin

Chongqing

Shanghai

Northeast wing
Population: 8,500,000

Changjiang River

Jialing River

Central city of Chongqing
Population: 6,500,000
Density: 1,170 per km²

20 km

Chongqing metropolitan area
Population: 11,300,000
Density: 800 per km²

Chongqing municipality
Area: 82,401 km²
Population: 28,000,000
Density: 350 per km²

Southeast wing
Population: 2,800,000

Chongqing rural–urban migration trend

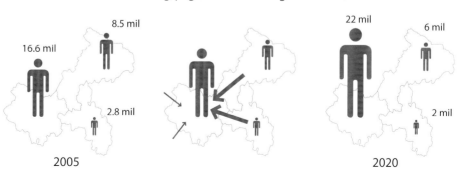

16.6 mil

8.5 mil

2.8 mil

2005

22 mil

6 mil

2 mil

2020

Within its metropolitan area, 11.3 million people reside, or 40 percent of the municipality's total population.

Due to its large area, however, the population density of Chongqing metropolitan area is low, at 800 people per square kilometer, while the central city of Chongqing has 6.5 million people and a population density of 1,170 people per square kilometer. Although about one-quarter of the Chongqing population is living in the nine districts of Chongqing's central city, its proportion of urban-core concentration is much lower than that of other metropolitan regions of China; for example, Beijing's is 76 percent, Shanghai's 63 percent (OECD, 2007).

Lower population density and spatially dispersed population decrease transportation efficiency by increasing travel distance, while also making it difficult to create a mass-transit system because of the lower catchment population for a viable public-transportation economy. Currently, three metro lines are in service in the central city of Chongqing with a combined capacity of 140 million in annual ridership. By 2020, Chongqing is planning to expand its metro system from 35 kilometers to 363.5 kilometers, with a total of seven rail lines, to ameliorate the pressure of its current public transportation demand. Simultaneously, Chongqing is adding 10,000 kilometers of paved rural road to provide access to public services such as schools and hospitals by 2012. Indeed, because of its extensive rural areas, Chongqing requires a concurrent developmental approach that responds simultaneously to urban and rural needs—heavy demand for mass-transit in the core urban area and public accessibility by roadways in the remote rural areas—which will inevitably mean higher energy consumption as compared to the other direct-controlled municipalities.

Chongqing is expecting internal migration of 5.5 million people over the next ten years, from the two east wings to the one-hour-drive circle (OECD, 2007), and this will accelerate urban–rural disparity in terms of public-transportation accessibility. The relocation of this population is becoming a big challenge, but at the same time it can be an opportunity for developing Chongqing. To afford this migration, Chongqing is already developing new urban areas within its metropolitan region, and here are four developments that can exemplify Chongqing's urban-development strategy: Nanping, Xiyong, Jiangjin, and Fuling.

Metro system comparison

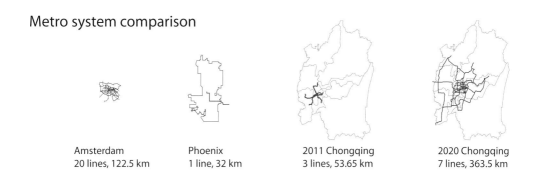

Amsterdam
20 lines, 122.5 km

Phoenix
1 line, 32 km

2011 Chongqing
3 lines, 53.65 km

2020 Chongqing
7 lines, 363.5 km

Chongqing urban development data

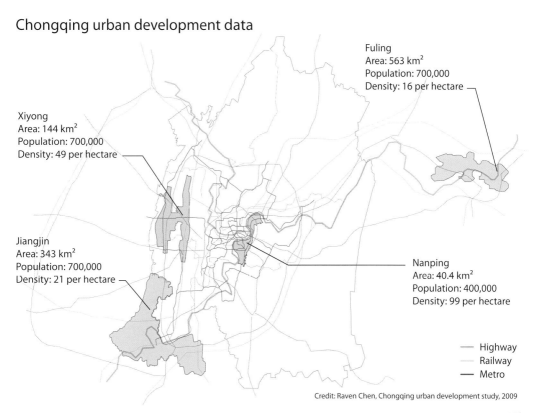

Fuling
Area: 563 km^2
Population: 700,000
Density: 16 per hectare

Xiyong
Area: 144 km^2
Population: 700,000
Density: 49 per hectare

Jiangjin
Area: 343 km^2
Population: 700,000
Density: 21 per hectare

Nanping
Area: 40.4 km^2
Population: 400,000
Density: 99 per hectare

— Highway
— Railway
— Metro

Credit: Raven Chen, Chongqing urban development study, 2009

Each development area has been designed to accommodate a population between 400,000 and 700,000. Since Nanping and Xiyong are within the nine central districts, the population density of each is relatively higher than the other two, at 99 people per hectare (one hectare = 10,000 square meters) and 49 people per hectare, respectively, while Jiangjin and Fuling have the relatively lower densities of 21 per hectare and 16 per hectare. Although these figures make the population density of the new urban-development areas appear very low—as if they are tending toward low-density urban sprawl—on closer inspection the reality turns out to be the opposite. Population density by building area of each development shows that density is increased from 1.3 times (Nanping) to 8 times (Fuling). This is due to the land-use plan of each development: only 15 percent of the land is used for building construction, on average, while the rest—37 percent on average—is used for agriculture. This means that most of the buildings are built with higher density features, such as a higher floor area ratio (FAR). Average FAR for residential and commercial use of each development is 215 and 500 percent, respectively. They are connected to the central city of Chongqing either by the railway or the highway network. Nanping and Xiyong are within Chongqing's subway extension plan, while Jiangjin and Fuling are mostly on the highway connection plan.

Transit-oriented development (TOD) is getting more attention in China as concern for the sustainability of urban growth is emerging. The city of Kunming, a central city of the Yunnan province in southwestern China, has developed its comprehensive city plan and urban public-transportation master plan based on the TOD strategy in cooperation with the city of Zurich, Switzerland (Fingerhuth, Joos, 2002). A network city has been proposed, connecting the urban core with satellite towns along the existing railway and public-transportation network systems. By planning the urban growth with higher population density allocated along this mass-transit network, Kunming's TOD scenario requires 101 square kilometers less development area, 11 percent decreased urbanization of fertile land, and also lowers the cost of new infrastructure due to less highway construction by 25 percent (Fingerhuth, Joos, 2002).

Chongqing has a similar approach to its metropolitan regional development: connecting existing and new urban centers with highway and railway systems, and designating these as development corridors. As seen in the graphic (page 157), most of the planned centers are

Chongqing new-development density comparison

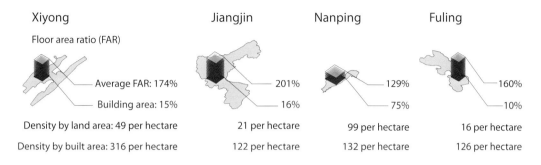

Xiyong	Jiangjin	Nanping	Fuling
Floor area ratio (FAR)			
Average FAR: 174%	201%	129%	160%
Building area: 15%	16%	75%	10%
Density by land area: 49 per hectare	21 per hectare	99 per hectare	16 per hectare
Density by built area: 316 per hectare	122 per hectare	132 per hectare	126 per hectare

Credit: Raven Chen, Chongqing Urban Development Study, 2010

Kunming development scenario comparison

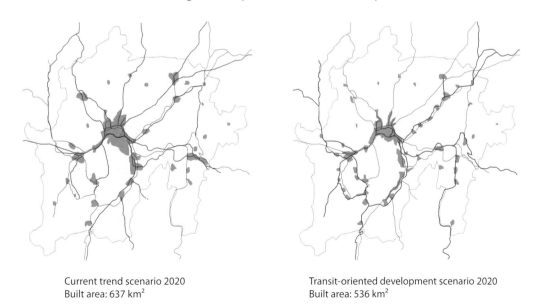

Current trend scenario 2020
Built area: 637 km²

Transit-oriented development scenario 2020
Built area: 536 km²

C. Fingerhuth, E. Joos, *The Kunming Project: Urban Development in China; A Dialogue*, 2002

interconnected by a highway system. This map suggests the likelihood of increased private automobile use and urban sprawl outside the development corridor, subsequent to the construction of access roads.

As an alternative to this plan, the Lean Linear City could be introduced as a maximized TOD strategy. Instead of a highway system, it proposes a public-transportation system—including regional railway, local light rail, cycling and pedestrian throughways—as a development corridor. In addition to making mass transit its core, Lean Linear City limits the urban-development footprint by its 200 x 200–meter modular plan. Each module can accommodate about 3,000 people and population density for each module is 160 people per hectare. The building footprint within a 200 x 200–meter module is 20 percent, achieving a density of 750 people per hectare. In comparison with Chongqing's new urban development, which averages 150 people per hectare, Lean Linear City has five times higher density. Each module has an average floor area ratio of 815 percent, which promotes three-dimensional growth of the module.

With higher FAR, the Lean Linear City module would have more floor space within its building footprint and density by floor space is 92 people per hectare. All areas of the 200 x 200–meter module are within five minutes' walking distance, and walking is documented to be the most efficient mode of transportation within a 250-meter radius in urban areas (Whitelegg, 1993). To afford new development accommodating 100,000 people, Lean Linear City would require 34 modules extending across approximately 6.8 kilometers, and all the modules in this Lean Linear development would be accessible within 20 minutes by bicycle or 30 minutes by local mass transit.

Even if many further studies need to be conducted, the point of view argued here is that the Lean Linear City model can be applied to Chongqing's new urban development and transportation plans to supply general guiding principles that increase sustainability through optimized population density and logistics. Furthermore, this model can be introduced to furnish design principles for any cities of the world confronting rapid urbanization.

Chongqing urban development scenarios

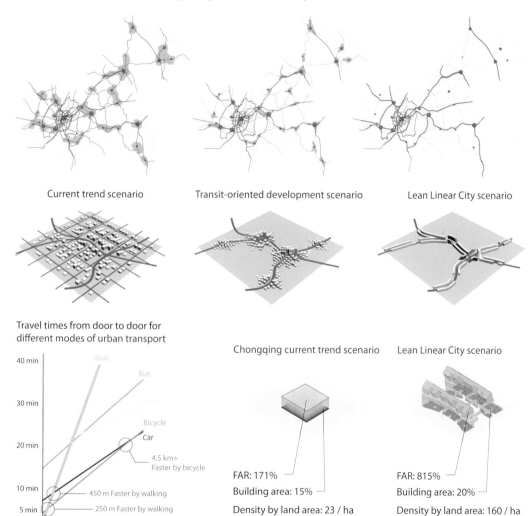

Current trend scenario

Transit-oriented development scenario

Lean Linear City scenario

Travel times from door to door for different modes of urban transport

40 min

Walk

Bus

30 min

Bicycle

20 min

Car

4.5 km+ Faster by bicycle

10 min

450 m Faster by walking

5 min

250 m Faster by walking

1 km 2 km   5 km

Source: J. Whitelegg, *Transportation for a Sustainable Future: The Case for Europe*, 1993

Chongqing current trend scenario

FAR: 171%

Building area: 15%

Density by land area: 23 / ha

Density by built area: 151 / ha

Lean Linear City scenario

FAR: 815%

Building area: 20%

Density by land area: 160 / ha

Density by built area: 750 / ha

Mixed-use development: utilities infrastructure, recreation, and constructed surrogate ecologies

Neo-Nature and the Evolution of Space

Adam Nordfors

Try to find an internet user who has not peered at his or her home or city from on high through the crystal ball of interactive satellite images. With a sweep of the hand this same voyeur-voyager can hover above the central Sahara, blurredly scroll to northern Siberia, and link to a marked location in the mountain ranges of the Antarctic. Wilderness areas have been effectively remapped in the consciousness as "places of lower resolution." Without a doubt, the human relationship to the planet has reached a milestone in its maturation. With friction of distance virtually dissolved, we can now survey what we behold. We see patterns including the nested web of grayish city sprawl, the endless mathematically delineated patchwork-carpet of pivot irrigation in the American midwest, and the constellations of lights that fill the night. Humankind's reputation as shaper of the environment is apt; the International Soil Reference and Information Centre (ISRIC) in the Netherlands estimated that by 1991 more than 7.5 million square miles of land had been degraded—an area roughly the size of Canada and the United States combined—yet built environments are continually designed and implemented in an industrial-era mindset that conceives of the human as separate from nature, as if they were two separate systems. The time for new land-use alternatives, which embrace our best collective abilities and technology, is now: land use that rivals the most sophisticated technology in aesthetics, productivity, efficiency, and utility. In his book *Nature's Metropolis* (1992), William Cronon proposes that the city and its surrounding rural setting are intrinsically connected, direct expressions of one another. After more than a century of impressive yet unintentionally destructive place-making, can we begin to create urban contexts that sculpt their immediate and regional surroundings in a manner that meets the needs of their human inhabitants while facilitating existing ecologies and fostering the rehabilitation of areas previously degraded? An era not of accelerated environmental atrophy, but one of orchestrated genesis, architecture as ecological generator? The Lean Linear City is poised both in form and philosophy to provide such an alternative. To begin to envision the fleshing out of a symbiotic multiuse habitat, we must take account of the components with which we are working.

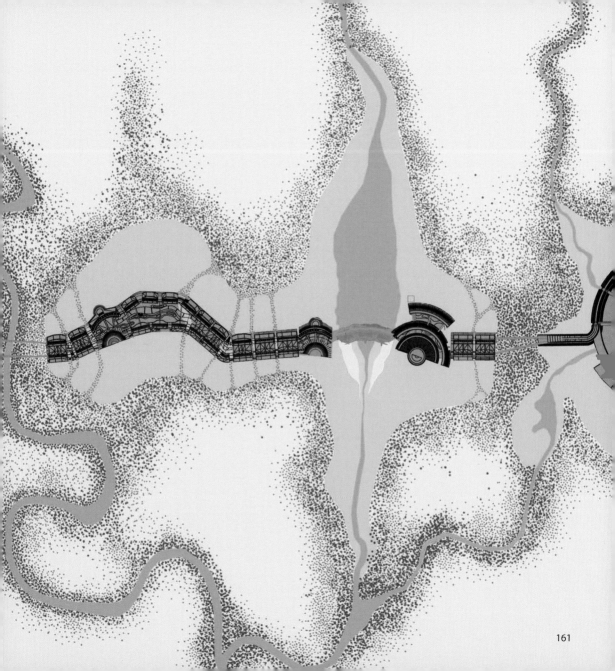

Ecosystem Services

It is no modern revelation that we as a species are dependent on earth and its natural systems. This concept has been in our collective memory in one form or another, transmitted by folktales, myths, and even a few religions, since the beginning of human history. In 2004, over one thousand scientists from around the world came together under the United Nations' Millennium Ecosystem Assessment to formalize the term "ecosystem services" as the commonly accepted scientific umbrella under which the processes and resources necessary for the continuation of human existence ultimately depend. "Ecosystem services" have to do with more or less everything, but the UN-delineated categories include:

- *Provisioning.* Food systems (fisheries, fertile soils, rangeland, etc.), the accumulation and purification of water, and the availability of raw materials.
- *Regulating.* Carbon sequestration, climate mitigation, regulating of global energy systems such as intact wetlands buffering coastlines, and intact permeable natural areas regulating annual flood events.
- *Providing habitat.* Appropriately sized, established natural areas performing nutrient cycling, providing habitat for biodiversity and its countless benefits, such as pollinators,

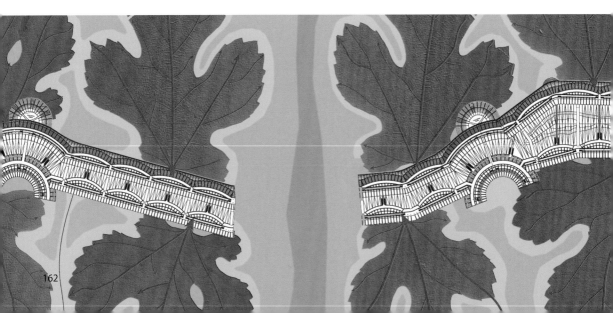

pharmaceuticals, etc.

• *Cultural services.* Cultural, intellectual, and spiritual inspiration, scientific discovery, and recreation.

In essence, these categories have been cornerstones of arcology theory since Paolo Soleri's early writings, a whole-systems approach to integrating architecture and ecology through the preservation and inclusion of the raw. The potential mutual benefits, both obvious and unforeseeable, are built into an unwavering philosophy of habitat design. In the form of Lean Linear City we find unique opportunity for the creation of high performance land-use systems through infrastructure-oriented design. By increasing the interface ratio of structure to open space, connecting and reassigning the inevitable outputs of "city"—such as waste water, thermal energy, and nutrient loads—to adjacent appropriately scaled sustainable systems becomes feasible; the management of what is seen as waste becomes part of an evolved feedback loop of human resource management. As in the architecture of the central structures, land-use efficiency is attained through multifunctionality of form; a poetic integration of infrastructure, recreation, and living systems within a walkable one-kilometer apron of sustainably used land.

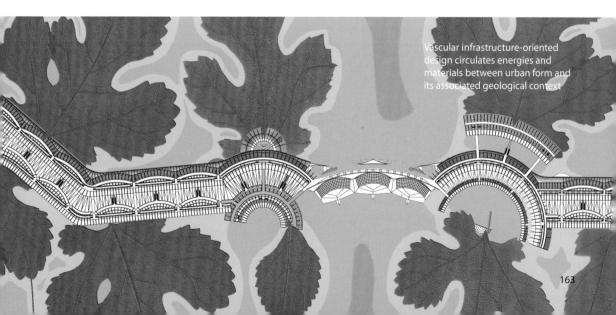

Vascular infrastructure-oriented design circulates energies and materials between urban form and its associated geological context

163

Animal Aspects of Architecture

Man versus nature—a classic struggle we have undertaken for millennia through the replacement of wilderness with tamed, predictable, and less risk-laden spaces for humans to flourish. Yet, in our current era of mass urban migration and megacities, we are beginning to sense something has gone seriously awry. Perhaps it is a haunting hollowness resulting from an unfulfilled ancestral biophilia, or the growing awareness of rapid biodiversity loss and the environmental instability associated with the deconstruction of tenuous matrices of ecosystems on which we depend. As human populations expand, facilitated by twentieth-century design models of development, habitat continues to be lost at an alarming rate. The increasing occurrence of large wild animals in rapidly growing cities (e.g., moose, coyote, bear) is a clear indicator of the phenomenon. These easily identified and media friendly macro-organisms act as barometers of the deeper problem at hand. As habitat decreases, so too does its associated biodiversity on both macro and micro scales. As earth's systems have fluctuated through the eons, biological resiliency has continued to endure through ecological complexity.

To continue to ignore the problem of decreasing biodiversity is to continue down a clearly self-destructive path as a species. A collective leap is required to perceive humans as a vital component of nature and an active participant in its evolution, and the reality of human habitat as a multispecies habitat, symbiotically integrated into the ecologies with which we have co-evolved. Where do we comfortably overlap? Where do we need to give each other space? What aspects of our respective environments can we share to the greater good of all?

A logical place to begin is in the open spaces typically set aside for recreation. While a definition of "meaningful recreation" may vary greatly from person to person, its importance to our wellbeing is becoming increasingly clear. For some it is time spent socializing in busy environments or delving into a novel, yet nearly everyone is pleased to enjoy a good walk in the park. The benefits of outdoor activity have become so evident that access to this resource is considered by progressive societies as crucial to public health and welfare. Socially there are the positive effects of community building, childhood development, and a decrease in overall psychological stress. Involvement in outdoor activity also creates a healthier population, alleviating pressures on the healthcare system. Businesses catering to recreation through

Landscape / infrastructure section

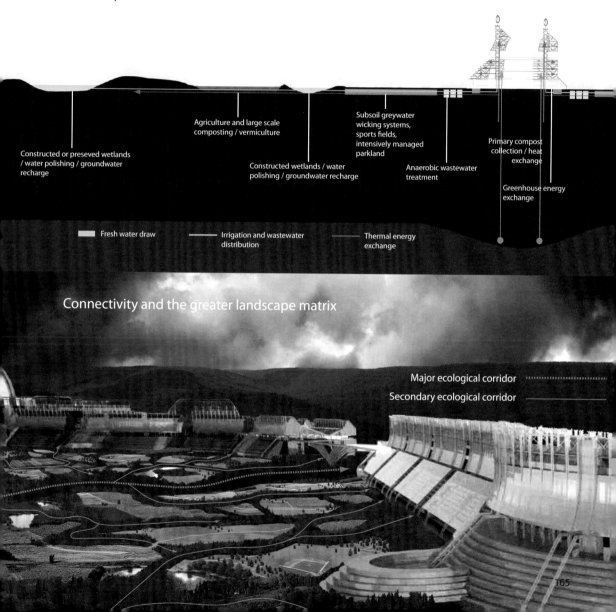

Constructed or preseved wetlands / water polishing / groundwater recharge

Agriculture and large scale composting / vermiculture

Constructed wetlands / water polishing / groundwater recharge

Subsoil greywater wicking systems, sports fields, intensively managed parkland

Anaerobic wastewater treatment

Primary compost collection / heat exchange

Greenhouse energy exchange

Fresh water draw

Irrigation and wastewater distribution

Thermal energy exchange

Connectivity and the greater landscape matrix

Major ecological corridor

Secondary ecological corridor

the sales and rental of sports equipment, fishing supplies, and training programs also help to create jobs. Environmentally we see a heightened awareness of nature fostering a sense of accountability in wildlife and habitat management and preservation. Clearly the presence of open space is mutually beneficial both to human society and its greater environmental context.

In the instance of Lean Linear City, a new potential for ecosystem inclusion in human habitat emerges. Rather than retroactively greening a vast impervious expanse nearly devoid of functional ecology, a comparatively miniscule threshold is left to resolve. The linear footprint allows for landscape corridors to strategically bypass the city, reducing disruption of core habitat while promoting a spectrum of appropriate interaction with urban existence. Solutions within the system occur in three modes:

- *Compressed urban forms.* Leaving expanses of diverse natural habitat intact through the creation of dense, human-scaled, high performance urban forms.
- *Local patterning.* Right of way for ecological connectivity through patches and corridors.
- *Tectonic inclusion.* The creation of wildlife habitat through augmented architectural form. Rather than simply designing around problematic elements of the natural world, we can actively encourage those elements that enhance our environment (e.g., bats in the bridges).

With the inclusion of the life sciences in the urban-planning process, both chemical and spatial tolerances of organisms may be quantified and applied in the design of the linear city.

An Agrarian-Urban Culture

We find ourselves in an era where the vast separation of food systems from the people dependent on them is becoming increasingly inefficient and illogical in a calorie-in, calorie-out model. Most experts believe agricultural output will need to increase 50–70 percent by 2050 in order to meet global demand while the needs of today are left wanting, with a billion people worldwide lacking access to adequate food supplies. This reality comes to us at a time of growing uncertainty over the long-term value and suitability of conventional agribusiness practice. Its dependence on oil supply and its vulnerability to political instability result in market volatility and inaccessibility to developing regions. Environmentally, the system proves even worse. Decades of systematic spraying for insects and weeds has brought us into an arms race with "superweeds" and "superpests," organisms that routinely develop resistances to our strongest chemical controls, necessitating higher potencies. Although these chemicals are generally tested and approved by governing bodies, corporate litigation massages the terminology and acceptable limits of chemical exposure until access to useful information becomes shrouded in nearly impenetrable layers of jargon. And though chemicals are tested individually, there is no possible means to determine the impact of the cocktails created in surface runoff, groundwater, and ultimately watersheds. At such a large scale, soil management also suffers greatly. Large expanses of monocrop systems degrade soils from class A to class C in a matter of years. Efficiency is sought in part by the simplification of the till-plant-reap cycle, achieved by removing nearly all crop residue at the end of each season, leaving soils easily workable in spring, yet bare and susceptible to erosion during dormant months. Soil loss represents one of the greatest threats to our survival as a species. What we have been trained to refer to as "dirt" is in reality the thin membrane that connects the mineral and organic worlds—a complex micro-ecology that serves as the key to the miraculous chemical exchanges which facilitate life as we know it. An impressive resource indeed, yet marginalized in our lexicon and our consciousness, we see it wash down our rivers and streams at increasing rates. The result can be observed in the growing dead zone of the Gulf of Mexico, where the Mississippi deposits its annual springtime load of nutrient-laden agricultural runoff.

The environmental impact goes beyond our soil reserves, rivers, and oceans. By blanketing our landscapes in region-wide monocrops we destroy an incomprehensible amount of ecological connectivity, natural habitat, and biodiversity. Entire ecosystems and their functionality are displaced, along with their ability to sustain life, mitigate climate, and retain and filter water. This phenomenon is unfortunately expanding at an alarming rate as existing farmland is displaced by urban sprawl, pushing food systems into our remaining intact forests, grasslands, and floodplains. Given that North America and regions of Europe are the heartlands of the large-scale petroleum-based agribusiness revolution, they provide observable, quantifiable examples of its functionality and impact as a land-use strategy. Cheap, abundant food is the crown jewel of the system at a long-term cost that remains alarmingly high environmentally,

Properly managed landscape-scale
ecological corridors double as
immediately available recreation
areas and places of research

economically, and socially. In the case of the United States, a nation built under the philosophical notion of the virtue of the gentleman farmer, entire regions of family farms have been driven off by large corporate farms run by a handful of people operating enormous equipment—the latter generally beyond the financial reach of the family farmer. Ironically, the high rate of unemployment continues to be an increasing problem, both financially and psychologically, in these same regions. Rapidly urbanizing developing countries in Asia and Africa often do not have systems in place to adopt this model of agricultural prosperity. Access to infrastructure, equipment, agricultural chemicals, and petroleum are limiting factors. Yet these are the areas most in need of immediate solutions to inadequate supplies of diverse, nutritive agricultural products. Along with hunger comes instability, making the issue of agriculture clearly a global human concern (see Olivier De Schutter, "Agroecology and the Right to Food" in References). The perpetuation of petroleum-based systems of high-yield crops, engineered disease-resistant varieties, and the use of poisonous chemicals seems to be a significant gamble as a long-term solution.

Economically the corporate farm model puts high profits in the hands of very few while entire regions of underemployed communities struggle to deal with the environmental degradation left in their wake. As consumers we are left with fewer varieties of produce of decreasing quality. In the past hundred years the United States has lost an estimated 97 percent of the genetic diversity of its food crops due to the shift towards varieties best suited to the rigors of long distance trucking and aesthetic consistency. As a result of growing concern, new models of farm economics are emerging in the United States in the form of Community Supported Agriculture and other forms of subscription farm operations where risk as well as surplus is distributed amongst members. In this approach middlemen are removed from the system, driving down costs, and access to diverse local food grown with sustainable methods is expected. With intact soil ecologies, greater fertility, and overall efficiency, many of these farms are able to match or outperform conventional large-scale agriculture in kilograms per square meter of food and fare much better in terms of nutritional values. Examples of other successful small-scale sustainable agriculture systems can be found in modern Cuba, which turned to sustainable farming practices following sudden devastating shortages of food supplies, agricultural chemicals, and farm machinery in the mid 1980s. In the 2005 publication *CPULs:*

Continuously Productive Urban Landscapes, Andrew Viljoen documents and describes the success of the nation's collective efforts in providing critical access to food via a spectrum of urban garden and farm models. Along with their implementation came jobs, reduced dependency on agricultural inputs, and a heightened awareness of standards of food quality.

In light of the long list of unsavory strings attached to modern corporate agriculture and the land-use tactics it employs, the notion of the oneness of human habitat, country and city, as advocated by the Lean Linear model, rings clearer by the moment. Food production is both our largest consumer of land and our collective means of survival. The solution to our impending global food supply shortage must be an elegant combination of approaches at varied scales, like all natural systems, gaining resiliency through its diversity. Within these models a movement toward local production to the greatest extent possible must be a criterion. The logistics of Lean Linear City provide a logical platform on which a new model of intensive sustainable agriculture may take root in our rapidly urbanizing world. With Lean Linear's vertical agricultural production via the greenhouse energy-apron and the inclusion of outdoor food production along the two-kilometer apron of sustainably used land, the symbiotic partnership between urban communities and immediately adjacent living soil ecologies reaches not only a new cultural significance, but also a scale previously unknown. An immediate symbiotic relationship between urban dweller and nature; nutrient rich compost, water and thermal energy from the urban waste stream creating matrices of enhanced high-performance agriculture and natural systems, exchanged for ecosystem services and high quality food. Such forms of integration will significantly alleviate reliance on industrial agriculture. As the next logical step in a spatial reformulation, it calls for a new paradigm of research, development, and implementation of environmentally and economically resilient models for food systems that are appropriate to diverse scales, climates, and ecological conditions. To begin to combine such systems with other human and ecological land uses on a large scale is truly to begin a new era of human innovation in how we occupy space as a species. As the natural systems in place and enduring long before us, our constructed environments, including food production, urban form, and their associated waste and nutrient cycling, will need to mimic such elegant complexity to give our civilizations true resiliency; a merger with the existing through a human-borne, human-amplified Neo-Nature.

Lean Linear City Landscape

Charles Anderson

The Lean Linear City is built on the principles of Emotional Urbanism, which elevate the human emotional craving for aesthetic beauty in the creation of ecologically sustainable landscapes. Lean Linear couples exquisite urban design with sustainable urban ecology through the integration of art, architecture, and landscape.

Natural systems are the basis of engaging, flexible, and beautiful Emo-Urbanism. They evolve to meet the changing programmatic needs of communities and continually resonate with their aesthetic desires. Inefficient and banal design wastes resources because it does not meet the long term needs of the community and inevitably falls into disuse and demolition. Aesthetically beautiful landscapes are not just follies for the eye, but essential to the culture of its inhabitants—and therefore sustainable.

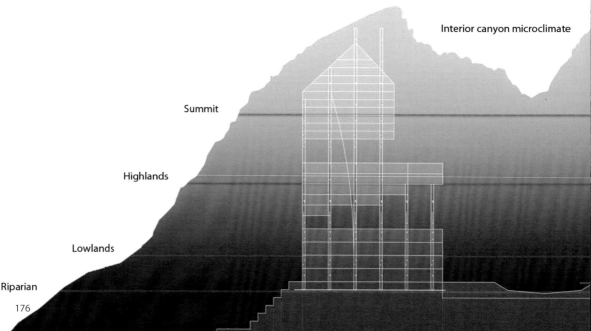

Interior canyon microclimate

Summit

Highlands

Lowlands

Riparian

The Lean Linear City forms a mountainous landscape of rising buildings supporting diverse alpine plant communities and lowland valleys of communal open space. Natural processes and the elevation-related microclimates of its infrastructure are the basis of the design.

The vertical gradient of the architecture influences the landscape plant communities and gardens throughout the city. The lowest areas are the most sheltered and have the greatest amount of available water. The highest part of the structures is characterized by wind desiccation, less available water, and higher temperature fluctuations. These varied conditions influence the plant communities and how the human community takes advantage of the evolving landscape. Much as the artist Robert Smithson responded to the entropy of nature by accepting and expressing environmental processes in his works, as with Spiral Jetty (1970) in Utah, the landscape of Lean Linear adapts to reflect the multitude of cultural and physical conditions that arise over time.

Sculpted volumes penetrate the façade of the buildings to allow for a vertical landscape of trees within the building. These openings in the architectural mass are sited to take advantage of solar access, views, and ceremonial and celestial events. This enhances the integration of the on-the-ground landscapes with the terra level, a mid-level landscape and transportation corridor, which brings large-scale landscape to a midpoint in the architecture and higher. Openings in the façade will allow intermittent landscape above and below the terra level. The sculptural carving of the building creates landscape possibilities that enrich life high above the land.

Transportation arteries connect all the life-sustaining places of the linear city with a central focus on pedestrian circulation, conveniently tied to local, regional, and world transport systems. Pedestrian connections knit each side of the module together with a series of bridges, which traverse the grand central landscape at the core of each module.

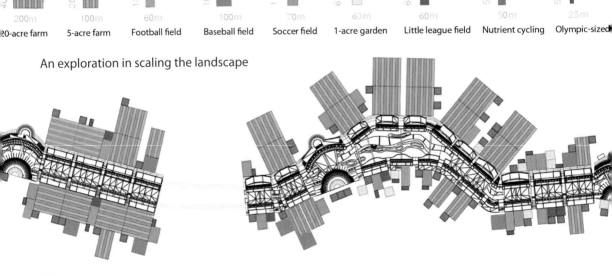

400m	200m	137m	100m	110m	63m	60m	50m	50m
200m	100m	60m	100m	70m	63m	60m	50m	25m
20-acre farm	5-acre farm	Football field	Baseball field	Soccer field	1-acre garden	Little league field	Nutrient cycling	Olympic-sized

An exploration in scaling the landscape

The central landscape supports extensive water harvesting, nutrimental gardens, and a vast array of civic and recreation spaces. Native riparian plants assist with biofiltration and remediation of storm-water runoff and gray-water harvesting. This flexible, dynamic, ecologically based landscape furthers our connections to its context by supporting wildlife with enhanced habitat corridors within and outside the architecture.

The landscape on the outer edges of each module is a combination of preservation lands, agriculture, and large-scale recreational facilities. Seeing the architecture as a setting for readily accessible urban open space ensures a variety of landscape expressions that arise from the culture and the site context to enrich and reconnect our lives to the natural evolving ecological processes. Emotional urbanism insists that the landscape be vital, indigenous, and appropriate to its context.

In all places of Lean Linear City, humans share the landscape with all other life, finding the perfect place to inhabit. Simply put, the hummingbird is as at home as humans are in this evolving, yet familiar, urban-agrarian city.

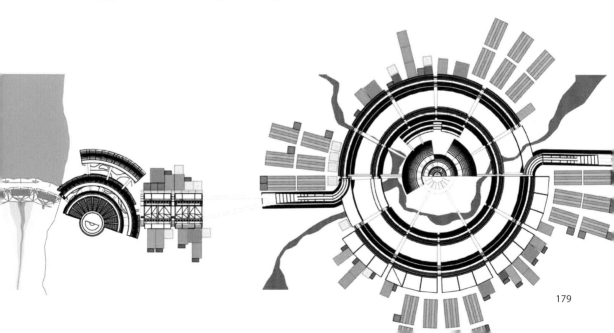

Cognition of Urban Space

Scott Riley

When London cabbies are asked to drive from one part of London to another, they know the best route to take. They have to. As part of their training, they have taken months to memorize the essential map of London, covering every street within a six-mile radius of Charing Cross. The information is apparently packed into the hippocampus, a region of the brain known to handle spatial navigation. Each cabbie, in an admittedly loose usage of words, recreates the map of London in his or her brain, complete with pub names, theater locations, and optimal routes.

The Los Angeles metropolitan area covers approximately 4,850 square miles of terrain (12,562 km²). It is too big to be known, too vast to be memorized. Each person's brain limits the conquest of this area to subsets: where one lives, where one works, how one commutes, where one visits the ocean. A portion of Santa Monica (where one lives) is joined to a smaller portion of downtown Los Angeles (where one works) by a variety of local roads and a section of interstate highway (how one commutes). These areas of inclusion are surrounded by much larger areas of exclusion; in fact, were it not for the areas of exclusion one could not negotiate the oceanic realm of the metropolitan area.

The use of the vertical axis in Los Angeles is limited; each person's map exists predominately in two dimensions, resulting in a flat latticework of pathways illuminated with overlapping memories of past and present streets.

In *t zero* Italo Calvino describes New York City as though it were a crystal (in the story titled "Crystals"). Who better than Calvino to decipher the inner workings of Manhattan? Most avenues and streets intersect at right angles, the skyscrapers rise vertically as do the elevators within, each level is further defined by right and left turns down linear corridors. What is important is not just the crystalline nature of this arrangement; Calvino is pointing out the not-so-obvious: the experience of this arrangement creates in the brain a crystalline map. Even when one is removed from the island of Manhattan, the map remains.

Charing Cross

6 miles

LONDON

LOS ANGELES

The mental mapping of Manhattan contains areas of inclusion and exclusion similar to those of Los Angeles, save for this difference: on Manhattan, the areas of exclusion rise vertically from the streets. The stacked pancake layers of each building are invisible to all save those who enter them. Each layer of each building is known, but no one knows all the layers. Each person has his or her own crystalline map, but each map is unique. When the individual maps are overlaid one upon another common terrain appears: the avenues, streets, subways, and parks, public zones of movement and relaxation that exist within the larger, often vertical, composite city.

Within the headquarters of the Ford Foundation in New York, an atrium of trees, water features, and natural light rises to the sky, providing an interior volume removed from the city (KRJDA). Within the Hong Kong and Shanghai Bank Headquarters an inner atrium creates an urban volume of bridges, walkways, elevators, and glass. It is as if the building has been turned inside out, as though one has entered a new definition of exterior, an exterior within (Norman Foster and Partners).

Modern buildings throughout the world routinely incorporate theaters, shopping malls, ice-skating rinks, even skiing slopes into their interior spaces. The stacked-pancake skyscraper has evolved into a more exciting definition of volume: extruded space. Although grand interiors have precedents in the architecture of religion and entertainment, many of these modern constructions exist as a part of a living environment of hotels, apartments, offices, cafes, schools, and parks. They are, in a manner of speaking, worlds unto themselves, and they present challenges to their designers, inhabitants, and visitors in terms of spatial definition and the corresponding inner mapping that accompanies the external world.

The renderings of Soleri's Lean Linear Arterial Arcology depict a redefinition of urban experience; locations once exterior to buildings now exist within. The walkways and bicycle paths are within, the fountains and flowing water are within, the cafes, restaurants and landscaping are within, storefronts are within, light rail transportation systems connecting the above are within. Even the street is within, reformed in multiple levels of pedestrian interaction, some at the base of the structure and others twelve stories above. The raised pedestrian level, called Terra, is in effect a lifting of the land into the body of the interior. It will serve as a base from

MANHATTAN

HSBC

183

which buildings rise; it will serve as a level of communion, public and accessible, not an atrium specific to a particular building but rather a place of transit, of cafés, of evening strolls, all contained within the urban form.

Lean Linear Arterial Arcology will be a challenge for those who develop the city. Rules of ownership and finance will be stretched or reinvented. Boundaries once physical will become technical. Rooftops will become walkways; wetlands will become inner-city parks. There will be similarities to the great metropolitan cities, with their subterranean trains burrowing beneath buildings, their avenues of electricity, water, waste and information flowing beneath the streets. But in Lean Linear Arterial Arcology such pathways will exist not beneath structures but within structures; right of ways will have to be redefined, service routes will be creatively invented or will cause undue discomfort to those who manage the living systems supporting urban life.

Ultimately the design, financing, construction and management complexities of Lean Linear Arterial Arcology will be seen not as obstacles but as hurdles, hurdles that can be crossed if the citizenry has the desire to cross them. What will remain, however, is the question of how, and how well, the populace will conceptualize their new surroundings. How will they map their journeys? How will they recognize and describe locations? How will they negotiate the circulation routes that, though they exist in real space, must by necessity be recreated in the mind?

Not everyone has the faculty for thinking in 3-D. One ought not assume that individuals will feel at home when their homes both rise and fall from the terra-level streets. The structure of the Arterial Arcology and the conceptualization of that structure will form a new frontier in the individual and collective cognition of urban space. That cognition will need to be fostered, nurtured, developed. In the process of evolving cognition we will need our London cabbies, not to deliver us to our destinations but to teach us how to find our way.

LEAN LINEAR CITY

References and Credits

Artibise, Yuri, Grady Gammage Jr., and Nancy Welch. "Transformation into Big City Has Benefits, Burdens." A*rizona Republic*, Sept. 26, 2008.

Bai, Z. G., R. de Jong, G. W. J. van Lynden. "An Update of GLADA: Global Assessment of Land Degradation and Improvement." ISRIC World Soil Information report. Wageningen, The Netherlands, August 20, 2010. http://www.isric.org.

Buehler, Ralph, and John Pucher. "Cycling to Sustainability in Amsterdam." *Sustain: A Journal of Environmental and Sustainability* Issues 21 (Fall/Winter, 2010): 36–40. Published by Kentucky Institute for the Environment and Sustainable Development.

Center for Sustainable Systems. *U.S. Environmental Footprint Factsheet*. Ann Arbor, MI: University of Michigan Press, 2009.

Chongqing Municipal Bureau of Statistics. *Chongqing Statistical Yearbook 2009*. Chongqing, China, 2009.

Cortright, Joe. *New York City's Green Dividend*. CEOs for Cities. April 2010. http://www.ceosforcities.org.

Cronon, William. *Nature's Metropolis: Chicago and the Great West*. New York: Norton, 1992.

De Schutter, Olivier. "Agroecology and the Right to Food." Report presented at the 16th Session of the United Nations Human Rights Council [A/HRC/16/49] by the Special Rapporteur on the right to food. March 8, 2011.

Fingerhuth, Carl, and Ernst Joos. *The Kunming Project: Urban Development in China; A Dialogue*. Basel: Birkhauser, 2002.

Kamal-Chaoui, Lamia, Edward Leman, and Zhang Rufei. *Urban Trends and Policy in China: Working Paper*. Organization for Economic Co-operation and Development, 2009.

Lv, Zhi-qiang, et al. "Monitoring of Urban Sprawl Using Geoprocessing Tools in the Shenzhen Municipality, China." *Environmental Earth Science* 62 (2011): 1131–41.

McKinsey Global Institute. *Preparing for China's Urban Billion*. Shanghai: McKinsey and Company, 2009.

National Association of Home Builders. *Housing Facts, Figures, Trends, and Single-Family Square Footage by Location*. 2007.

Newman, Peter W. G., and Jeffrey R. Kenworthy. *Cities and Automobile Dependence: An International Sourcebook*. Brookfield, VT: Gower Technical, 1989.

Organisation for Economic Co-operation and Development, China Development Research Foundation. *Trends in Urbanisation and Urban Policies in OECD Countries: What Lessons for China?* 2010.

Organisation for Economic Co-operation and Development. *Chongqing Municipality's Development Strategy: Some Reflections from the International Experience of the Territorial Development Policy Committee of the OECD*. 2007.

Owen, David. *Green Metropolis: Why Living Smaller, Living Closer, and Driving Less are the Keys to Sustainability*. New York: Riverhead, 2009.

Soleri, Paolo. *The Sketchbooks of Paolo Soleri*. Cambridge: MIT Press, 1970.

United Nations Department of Economic and Social Affairs, Population Division. *World Urbanization Prospects*. 2009 revision. New York, 2010.

United Nations Department of Economic and Social Affairs, Population Division. *World Urbanization Prospects: BRICS and Selected OECD Countries*. 2007 revision. New York, 2008.

United Nations Environment Programme, Global Assessment of Human-induced Soil Degradation, (GLASOD). ISRIC World Soil Information. Wageningen, The Netherlands, 1991. http://www.isric.org.

United Nations Population Fund. *UNFPA State of World Population 2007: Unleashing the Potential of Urban Growth*. New York, 2007.

U.S. Census Bureau, A. Wilson, and J. Boehland. "Small Is Beautiful: U.S. House Size, Resource Use, and the Environment." *Journal of Industrial Ecology* 9, no. 1–2 (2005): 277–87.

U.S. Census Bureau. American Community Survey One-Year Estimates, 2009; *Workers 16 Years and Over: Public Transportation (excluding taxicab)*, 2009.

Viljoen, André, Katrin Bohn, and Joe Howe, eds. *CPULs: Continuous Productive Urban Landscapes; Designing Urban Agriculture for Sustainable Cities*. Oxford: Architectural Press, 2005.

Whitelegg, John. *Transportation for a Sustainable Future: The Case for Europe*. London: Belhaven, 1993.

World Wildlife Fund. *Living Planet Report 2010; Biodiversity, Biocapacity and Development*. 2010.

Pages 1, 146, 147, 194, 195, 196. Rendering credit: Tomiaki Tamura.

Pages 4, 5, 158, 159, 161, 162, 163, 165, 168, 169, 172, 173. Rendering credit: Adam Nordfors.

Pages 10, 11, 70, 71. Rendering credit: Youngsoo Kim and Jose Masaoy.

Pages 14, 21, 27, 29, 33, 37, 78–81, 86, 88–93, 98, 99, 102, 106, 107, 119, 125–129. Photo credit: Youngsoo Kim.

Page 16. Photo credit: NASA, China at night, Beijing-Tianjin, China, 2010.

Pages 17–19, 23, 28, 31, 33, 35–39, 41, 43–49, 104, 121–123, 131, 149, 151, 153, 155, 157, 181, 183, 185. Illustration credit: Youngsoo Kim.

Pages 44–46. Lean Linear City module in architectural cardboard constructed by architects Flavio Borrelli and Antonio Chelen Guerra, August 2011.

Pages 50–55, 57, 60, 61, 65–69, 73–77, 82, 83, 100, 101, 116, 117, 136, 137, 140, 178, 179, 186, 187. Rendering credit: Youngsoo Kim.

Pages 58, 59, 62, 63, 112, 113. Rendering credit: Youngsoo Kim and Adam Nordfors.

Pages 94, 95, 97. Illustration credit: World Wildlife Fund.

Page 108. Photo credit: Facebook.

Page 133. Credit: Prof. Ignacio San Martin, Phoenix city expansion and area comparison study, 2000.

Pages 135. Photo credit: Randy Olson and Melissa Farlow, 2009.

Pages 140, 141. Illustration credit: Paolo Soleri.

Pages 153, 155. Credit: Raven Chen, Chongqing Urban Development Study, 2010.

Page 174–177. Illustration credit: Charles Anderson.

Arcosanti Planning Department staff members have contributed to the design development of the Lean Linear City project.

About the Authors

Paolo Soleri (b. 1919, Turin, Italy) was awarded his Ph.D. in architecture from Torino Polytechnico in 1946. He came to the United States in 1947 to pursue a fellowship with Frank Lloyd Wright at Taliesin. In 1956 he settled in Scottsdale, Arizona, where he established the not-for-profit Cosanti Foundation, beginning a lifelong commitment to research and experimentation in urban planning. The foundation's major project, Arcosanti, has been under construction near Cordes Junction in central Arizona since 1970. The project is based on Soleri's concept of "arcology," architecture conceived in coherence with ecology.

Youngsoo Kim completed a joint master and bachelor degree in architecture with a concentration in urban design at the University of Arizona in 2008. After graduation, he was invited by Soleri to continue working in the Arcosanti Planning Department, overseeing projects such as the Lean Linear City design proposal. Kim's professional intention is to translate Soleri's Lean Linear model into practical applications for urban planning in developing countries that are experiencing rapid urbanization.

Charles Anderson is a landscape architect with over twenty years of experience in projects ranging from neighborhood parks to New York City's American Museum of Natural History. He has a strong background in public process and has completed many community projects. Anderson has a specific interest in expressionistic landscape restoration and in the development of urban ecologies. He earned his bachelor degree in landscape architecture from Washington State University and his master degree in landscape architecture from Harvard University's Graduate School of Design in 1985.

Adam Nordfors received his Journeyman Farmers Status from Maine Organic Farmers and Gardeners Association in 1997 before joining the Arcosanti project as land-use manager and agricultural workshop instructor. He has since gone on to study Geographic Analysis at Ryerson University and Landscape Architecture at Arizona State University, where he received his landscape architecture degree. Currently he teaches design studios and a course on alternative construction methods at ASU and works as a sustainable systems designer.

Scott Riley is a habitat coordinator for the Arcosanti project. He assisted the Cosanti Foundation on occasional projects beginning in 1973, and joined the staff in 2000. His work for Cosanti Foundation has extended to database design, project oversight, and habitat coordination.

Tomiaki Tamura joined the Cosanti Foundation in 1976, where he worked as a project coordinator, overseeing planning and construction of Arcosanti. As the director of the Soleri Archives, he has produced numerous exhibitions and publications. He graduated from Arizona State University with a master's degree in environmental planning.

Jeff Stein, AIA, award winning architect and writer, is president of the Cosanti Foundation. A longtime Soleri collaborator, Stein is both a graduate and former dean of the Boston Architectural College. He previously taught at architecture schools in the US and in Zurich, Switzerland, and Montpellier, France. He has authored numerous articles on architecture and energy issues and lectures widely about Arcosanti and urban design.

Lissa McCullough has worked with Paolo Soleri as his editor since 2005. She is an idependent scholar with a master's degree from Harvard University and a doctorate from the University of Chicago. She is now based in Los Angeles, having previously taught in the field of religious studies at New York University, Hanover College, and Muhlenberg College.

Index

A

agriculture 72
American dream 15, 18, 120, 134
Amsterdam 148, 150
arcology 8, 9, 30, 32, 118, 121, 144
arterial arcology 8, 9, 32
artery 32
automobile 31, 34, 120, 145, 148, 150, 156

B

better kind of wrongness 16, 24
biosphere 95, 106, 130

C

Calvino, Italo 180, 184
China 16, 18, 20, 29, 78, 150, 152, 154
Chongqing 150, 152, 154, 156
city 8, 15, 16, 20, 30, 32, 34, 90, 105, 120, 122, 124,
        128, 130, 134, 143, 144, 145, 148, 160, 182
civilization 20, 120, 122, 128, 132, 134
coherence 15, 24, 96, 105, 132
complexity 8, 26, 32, 104, 105, 106, 107, 109, 110
consumption 15, 31, 32, 72, 92, 95, 118, 132, 144,
        146, 148, 150, 152
Cronon, William 160
culture 8, 9, 18, 20, 24, 120, 122, 125, 128, 130, 132,
        134

D

"Do more with less" 86, 87
Doxiadis, Konstantinos 144

E

ecology 8, 15, 26, 118, 163
ecosystem 162

ecosystem services 162
Emotional Urbanism (Emo-Urbanism) 174
energy 22, 64
environment 16, 18, 72, 90, 118, 144, 145, 182
evolution 22, 32, 40, 42, 104, 107, 120, 130
exurbia 15, 16, 20, 22, 24, 134

F

floor area ratio 154, 156
food 26, 72, 87, 96, 118, 124, 146
Foster, Norman 182
frugal 95, 145

G

geometries 24, 26, 30, 40, 122, 134
gravity 22, 24
greenhouse 32, 34, 39, 72

H

hashi 9
habitat 24, 30, 32, 34, 72, 87, 96, 120, 130, 132
hermit 15
Homo faber 24, 26, 42, 132, 134
Homo sapiens 15, 26, 42, 95, 130
Hong Kong 29, 144, 182
horizontal hermitage 15
howness 20, 132
hyperconsumption 26, 96, 130, 132
hyperorganism 90, 106, 130, 134

K

Kunming 154

L

laboratory 24
landscape 166, 175, 177
lean alternative 26, 88, 92, 96, 98, 118, 145
Lean Linear Arterial Arcology 30, 182, 184

Lean Linear City 3, 5, 7, 8, 9, 11, 13, 36, 37, 39, 54, 56, 104, 142, 143, 145, 146, 147, 148, 156
lean society 87, 96
linear city 20, 30, 32, 40, 144
logistical efficiency 22, 148
logistical system 31, 56
logistics 20, 22, 24, 30, 32, 34, 120, 156
London 180, 184
Los Angeles 21, 180, 182

M

Manhattan 27, 90, 180, 182
mass transit 56, 144, 148, 150, 152, 154
materialism 15, 18, 26, 32, 87, 98, 132, 134
Mesa City 143, 144, 147
metastasis 15, 16, 20
miniaturization 103, 109, 110
mobility 20, 32
module 34, 36, 39, 40, 42, 48, 54, 156
mysterium tremendum 110

N

neo-nature 146, 160, 171
network 32, 42, 105, 108, 120, 154
New York City 27, 90, 98, 144, 180

O

organism 90, 104, 118, 120, 122, 123, 124, 130
Owen, David 144

P

park 34, 38, 54, 58, 62, 64
Phoenix 27, 29, 148, 150
photovoltaic 32, 40, 64
planet 8, 9, 15, 20, 22, 30, 40, 42, 96, 98, 104, 130, 132
planetary hermitage 15
presence 20, 24, 26, 30, 32, 96, 128, 130
proximity 22, 24, 120, 143, 148

public transportation 34, 144, 152

R

religare 118, 134
reform 18
reformulation 15, 24, 26, 30, 145

S

self-awareness 15
self-creation 26, 110, 130
self-reliant 32
single-family home 26, 88, 92, 96, 98, 118, 145
single-home hermitages 15
space geometries 24
structure 32, 40, 42, 56, 72, 184
suburban 16, 26, 34, 106
suburbia 15, 16, 20, 22, 34

T

transcendence 92, 95, 110, 130
transit-oriented development 154
transportation 20, 22, 34, 56, 144, 148, 150, 152, 154, 156, 184

U

urban effect 22, 104, 105, 110, 130, 134, 144
urban landscape 134, 145
urban module 34
urban ribbon 30, 32, 40, 42
urban sprawl 15, 31, 118, 145, 154, 156

V

vertebrate 40
vertical hermitage 15
volition 104, 118, 134

W

Western formula 18